Tom Bryan

and Other

Movers and Shapers

of

Early Fort Lauderdale

KEITH D. MITZNER

ISBN: 978-1-4834-2518-4 (sc)
ISBN: 978-1-4834-2517-7 (e)

Library of Congress Control Number: 2015902071

Lulu Publishing Services rev. date: 2/6/2015

Special Acknowledgements

The ensuing narrative is made possible by the Fort Lauderdale Historical Society archives. The clipping files contain unpublished notes and memorabilia plus locally printed records and old media reporting that are not otherwise readily available to the public. Of this collection, particular recognition must go to the columns of Wesley Stout. From 1952 to 1971 Mr. Stout wrote a daily column for the *Fort Lauderdale News* entitled the Beachcomber, collecting trivia "as a beachcomber gathers flotsam and jetsam." His local sources included the first settlers who were still on the scene: Tom Bryan, Mrs. Frank Oliver, Uncle Dick King, Bird and Louise King, Deacon Berryhill, Ivy Stranahan and various Cromarties, among others. These sources were also avid readers of Beachcomber columns, and they did not hesitate to provide corrections and amplifications that then fueled further columns. These personal recollections provide both anecdotal richness and clarity to the story line. The Fort Lauderdale Historical Society houses Stout's collection of scrapbooks containing all his columns. It has been a pleasure to mine this source, and I greatly appreciate the assistance, support and encouragement of the History Center staff.

Keith Mitzner
Fort Lauderdale, FL
January 2015

Contents

Opening Remarks

Fort Lauderdale is on so many Top Ten lists that it is impossible to keep up. No wonder! It is a marvelous place to live, work, and play. A small city that may never reach 200,000, it contains a major seaport and cruise terminal, a bustling international airport, a fabulous beach, a world-class yacht center, a gorgeous and inviting riverfront, a dynamic business community, plus a full array of cultural and entertainment options. It is an all-season place that is always exuding energy, and everything is only minutes away. The convenience factors here are unbelievable, and in moments of reflection one cannot help but wonder "How could something so well-done happen?"

The answer is in the people that brought it together. There was no master plan, but a vision and an overriding sense of teamwork. No one dominated for long. They worked hard, cooperated and collaborated to create a system, and they worked within it. It was so American, a dream that did come true. But up close it was a pretty humdrum story, like watching a busy ant colony. Efficient accomplishment masks the human element, and this narrative is an attempt to go beyond the chronology to provide a sense of the human dynamics that contributed to the foundations of Fort Lauderdale, the human drama.

Drama implies a stage, a setting, and cast with starring and supporting roles. I am also injecting myself into this production as the narrator, and I am speaking from Fort Lauderdale. When I say "we," I mean you and I; and when I say "here," I mean Fort Lauderdale. I have studied these pioneers to the point that I feel that I know them, and I want to share their stories. I am featuring two families in some detail: Tom Bryan and the family he came from; and Ed King and the young family he brought in. They are among the earliest real settlers, arriving when Fort Lauderdale was nothing but a trading post and a postal drop. Their subsequent lives were integral parts of the emerging community, and as such they are representative in many respects of what all the early settlers were experiencing. But Tom Bryan and Ed King were instigators, and each in his own way went well beyond the norm to make things and do things. Tom Bryan, in particular, stands out. His actions touched nearly every aspect of the emerging community, often in unique ways.

If Tom Bryan and Ed King were getting awards for star performance, they would have long lists of co-workers and supporters to thank, and they are both men who would do that. In their stead, I will acknowledge other important players in chapter 5, but special recognition must go to the group effort. No one individual drove the whole process. It really was a band of brothers that moved and shaped the emerging Fort Lauderdale. Everything that evolved was kept in the context of the common process and common good. That is the real legacy of the early settlers, because it is still that way.

Now, before going to the family stories, here is a brief description of the setting and circumstances that they would face upon coming in to this undeveloped territory.

1

Setting the Stage

The setting in 1890 was identified by its river, the New River. This river was short, unusually deep for Everglades drainage, and with no outlet. It was blocked from the sea by the coral barrier strip that separated the ocean from the landmass. This forced the river flow to disperse behind the barrier in an extensive inland waterway system that included a lake and massive mangrove swamps. Our focal point, then, is on the higher land about two miles inland from the Atlantic Ocean. This is roughly forty-five miles south of Palm Beach and about thirty miles north of Miami.

In 1890 the New River area had only one official resident, the keeper at the life-saving station—House of Refuge—at the beach. No one lived inland except for roving bands of Seminoles, not recognized by the government. The Seminole Wars had successfully eliminated earlier white settlements along the New River, but the Indians took refuge in the Everglades and never left. The only other significant remnant from that time was the name, Fort Lauderdale. A Major Lauderdale sent to engage the Indians in 1838 put up a thirty-by-thirty stockade and named it after himself. He and his volunteers departed in fewer than sixty days, but the name was recorded on government maps. When first mail service began in 1891 with a postal drop at the House of Refuge, the US Post Office perpetuated the Fort Lauderdale name as the postal address.[1]

Preliminary Actions
1870–1890

An 1870 land survey of the area now known as Broward County showed only a single piece of privately owned property, a square mile of the choicest high ground straddling the New River, more than a mile from the sea. This was called a Donation, a Spanish land grant going back to the eighteenth century and recognized by subsequent governments. This uninhabited square mile, known as the Frankee Lewis Donation, was bought in the early 1870s by William and Mary Brickell, not for any interest in the New River, but because it was included in the Brickell's purchase of a package of four land grants. The other three contained prime land along the Miami River, the Brickells' target. They settled there and founded the city of Miami.[2]

In the 1880s the ownership situation in the New River area flipped from mostly governmental to mostly private. Speculators and investors, who had never set foot on the land and had no such intention, snapped up large tracts. With a second wave of buyers in 1890, the Brickells in effect bought up the New River.[3] With a single purchase of five-and-a-half square-mile blocks extending west from their Frankee Lewis Donation, the Brickells controlled most everything in the area except the beach and mangrove swamps.

The Brickells were friends of Henry Flagler who was building lavish hotels and railroads in northern Florida in the 1880s. By 1890 Flagler's Florida East Coast (FEC) Railway was already heading south toward Palm Beach, and the Brickells were positioning themselves for an eventual extension to Miami.

Game-Changing Actions and Events
1890-1895

The New River area was left untouched for so long because it was not easily accessible. There were no roadways and no seaport. That changed in 1892 when a county road was built between Lantana—south of Palm Beach—and North Miami. The Bay Biscayne Stage Line, a mule-drawn hack, initiated three-day-a-week service on this route. It was a two-day trip. The overnight stop was at the New River at the ferry crossing. Bay Biscayne service began on January 24, 1893, and Frank Stranahan came in on the second stage on January 27 to establish and run the overnight camp and operate the ferry. This regular service quickly had the mail contract, so Frank's camp also became the post office and assumed the Ft. Lauderdale postal address from the House of Refuge at the beach.

The new road and camp created a serious issue for the Brickells, for the roadway bisected their prized Frankee Lewis Donation, prime land for development. The Brickells forced the issue with the county and in effect bribed Frank Stranahan to move his camp half a mile upstream. The Brickell's gave Frank ten acres of riverfront property adjacent to the donation's western boundary line. Frank moved his camp, and the roadway with ferry crossing was re-routed around the donation. This was probably all in place by January 1894. Once Frank Stranahan became a property owner, he upgraded his tourist accommodations and built a small store that served as post office as well as trading post. Frank's original customers were transients and Seminoles, but, for anyone new coming into the area, Stranahan's was the only place to go for anything. Frank's camp quickly became the nerve center and one-stop service center for the emerging community.[4]

An early patron of Stranahan's in 1893 was Hugh Taylor Birch. Birch was a very wealthy, reclusive businessman from Chicago looking for a personal sanctuary. By May 1893 Birch and his partner, John MacGregor Adams, had purchased the sixty acres abutting the House of Refuge to the north. In subsequent acquisitions

Birch kept ahead of investors and speculators until he controlled over three miles of the beach barrier strip, everything above the House of Refuge.[5] So, in very quick order in the emerging Fort Lauderdale, one outside party owned the river and another owned the beach, both parties holding on for the long term.

Lastly, a distant natural calamity provided a major stimulant for the development of Fort Lauderdale. A great freeze, actually back-to-back freezes of December 1894 and February 1895, wiped out the citrus industry and local economies of citrus-growing areas in northern Florida. The first freeze took the crop and the second took the trees. State citrus production plummeted from six million boxes of fruit per year to one hundred thousand boxes. Real estate values dropped accordingly. Many growers simply abandoned their groves. Refugees from this exodus provided much of the energy for early Fort Lauderdale.

The great freeze also unleashed a torrent of activity in the worlds of Henry Flagler and the Brickells. A rush of negotiations was concluded between February and June 1895 that would define Fort Lauderdale. On June 12 the two parties agreed on the details of the coming railroad. Mary Brickell held firm on her demand that the route would circumvent the Frankee Lewis Donation. She insisted that the tracks swing west to avoid the one-square-mile Frankee Lewis Donation altogether and pass through a one-square-mile Fort Lauderdale township that she designated west and adjacent to the donation. Flagler agreed to plat the town, build a station, develop streets, and promote the city in his advertising and publicity. In return the Brickells gave Flagler approximately 248 acres in town lots plus twenty-one acres of right-of-way. After excluding the river acreage from the town's square mile, the Brickells gave Flagler essentially half of the town property.[6]

The Setting
1895

The year 1895 is the real beginning date for Fort Lauderdale as we know it. The actual settlers who came here with the intention of putting down roots all traced their arrival back to 1895. Fortuitously, the framework for their town-to-be had already been determined by outside forces. Before the settlers could even get established, a village named Fort Lauderdale had been platted. It was a happy combination of factors for both the newcomers and the founding forces. Both were looking to the free enterprise system to achieve their goals. Success by the newcomers would mean success for the founding investors, and no one was eager to control. It was as if in 1895 the stage had been set and settlers came in with the invitation, "See what you can do with this!" The rest of this narrative is a description of their response to this challenge. Those early settlers did some amazing things.

2

Tom Bryan and the P.N. Bryan Family

Among the founding settlers of Fort Lauderdale, the family of Philemon Nathaniel Bryan was a notch above everyone else. They were not uppity—it was just the reality. Philemon had been founding mayor of New Smyrna, a coastal town 200 miles north. He had been a very successful merchant and owner of fruit groves, packinghouses, town buildings, a sawmill and cattle, among other things. His wife, Lucy, had not only raised a family, but for decades she had provided lodging to boarders and was an entrepreneur in her own right. Their two young sons Reed and Tom, schooled in hard work and making things happen, were both college graduates. They were a tight, effective and efficient team, and no other single force was more influential or important to the founding of Fort Lauderdale and Broward County than this powerhouse family. Once they were firmly established, they took the initiatives that propelled the village of Fort Lauderdale first to incorporated town and then county seat in little more than five years. It was a huge accomplishment that rather quickly faded into the noise of ensuing development, for the Bryans were not a political machine or dynasty. Their focus was on economic development. They were free-enterprisers to the bone, and they were sophisticated enough to understand the need for supportive structure in order to prosper. Once the structure was established, they participated and benefited as new waves of leadership took over. After that early surge of accomplishment the elder Bryans and son Reed faded from public view, but young son Tom continued in a role that alternated between public and private activities, and he was a force on the local scene for many years to come. There is not a high degree of name recognition for this family, but with the perspective of intervening decades we should be able to stand back and say the Philemon N. Bryan Family put Fort Lauderdale as we know it on the map.

The family of Philemon N. Bryan got its start in Volusia County, Florida. Philemon and Lucy Murray were married there in 1867. He was almost twenty-three and she was only fifteen. Philemon had served in the Confederate Army for most of three years, attaining the rank of First Sergeant, and had joined his family in Florida at the end of the Civil War. His father in 1864 had been the first settler in the village of Glencoe, just west of New Smyrna, and was in the process of establishing a farm and citrus groves. Philemon, the oldest surviving son, brought welcome energy to this project, and they prospered. The 1880 Federal Census finds a set of Bryan families living in Glencoe in a sequence of residences: **P.N.** (35) and Lucy (27), four daughters from six to twelve, two sons almost two and four, and two boarders, a teacher and a laborer; **Gadsden** (28), wife Mary (20), baby son, a servant and a boarder; and **Louis H.** (63), wife Georgia (30), son Franklin A (7), and a daughter (4). In the Occupation category, P.N. is listed as Farmer, brother Gad as Raising Cattle, and father Louis as Unoccupied. So, it would seem that Louis had retired, possibly in poor health, while P.N. as ranking family member was managing groves and other properties while Gad handled the cattle-raising part of the business. You will note that Louis Bryan's wife is younger than Philemon, a second marriage for Louis Bryan with two small children. The boy Frank will appear later in this narrative as an adult in Fort Lauderdale.[7]

Father Louis H. Bryan died in 1882, and most probably Philemon continued to manage and develop the family assets. By the 1885 Florida State Census the living arrangements and precinct number had changed, suggesting that all of the family had moved into New Smyrna though still living relatively close to each other. Philemon was now in a residence that accommodated seven children from three to seventeen, three servants and two boarders. Philemon is categorized as Merchant. So, by this time Philemon Bryan must have established his big general store in New Smyrna that according to family lore sold everything from sugar to saddles to clothing.

In the decade from 1885 to 1895 Philemon N. Bryan was in his prime, age forty-one to fifty-one. He was clearly a big operator, and the scraps of information we have suggest that he managed a small empire: a major retail store, commercial buildings, a sawmill, extensive citrus groves and packing houses, cattle and probably other farming. He was also a major force in getting New Smyrna incorporated as a town in 1887, and he became the first mayor. As Henry Flagler's Florida East Coast line (FEC) proceeded down the coast toward Daytona, P. N. Bryan lobbied early with Flagler to continue another fifteen miles to New Smyrna. Bryan became a major shipper on the FEC, and a friend of Flagler.[8]

But life was not perfect. The family had dealt with death and personal economic disaster before the calamitous freeze of 1894/1895. The Bryan's fourth daughter, Mary, died in 1886 at age twelve, and anyone who has experienced the loss of a child knows that this changes life perspectives for everyone in the family. A few years later, possibly around 1892, the uninsured Bryan store was wiped out in a fire. This would have been a shock in many respects, though the Bryans' diversified assets still provided income. In any case, adversities test family bonds, and the P. N. Bryan family seemed to have coped well, honing their skills for pulling together and supporting each other.

The family group as of 1885 would have made a nice picture with seven stair-step height children, ages 17, 15, 13, 11, 9, 7 and 3: four girls, Virginia, Eliza, Florence and Mary; two lads, Reed and Tom; and the baby Constance. Father Philemon was forty-one and mother Lucy was thirty-three. Mary died the following year, creating a four-year gap between the boys and older girls to match the four-year gap between the boys and baby Constance. The family likely functioned primarily in two sets, older girls and young boys, with the baby being spoiled by everyone. So the boys were teamed up early and probably had a special status in the family with high expectations and hopes.

Two rare anecdotes pertaining to Reed as a young lad give a glimpse into the Bryan family culture. Reed was very fond of horses and would go to the barn, grab the halter of one of the farm horses, lead it to a railing or other prop to assist him in jumping on, then proceed to ride around the property. The story implies there were falls and scrapes and other risks much to the consternation of his mother, but Reed persisted. In another example, Reed would side with the weakest and smallest in typical boyhood quarrels, and on one occasion gave a real licking to the town bully. The source of the information was undoubtedly Lucy or Philemon Bryan in a 1911 article about the Bryan Hotel, and more noteworthy than the specifics is the choice of incidents to exemplify perseverance and fair play. It also shows an appreciation for taking initiative, taking risks, expecting hard knocks, and ultimately prevailing in an objective.[9]

Hard work was the modus operandi for the family. The boys may have been special and little, but they were trained to take responsibility and be accountable. This contributed to a high degree of trust and confidence within the family, obvious later in the surprising level of responsibility that Philemon assigned to seventeen-year-old Tom in early Fort Lauderdale. But the Bryan family was more than an efficient team. There is a strong sense that they enjoyed each other, and sharing was an important component of their relationships, whether work or play, sorrow or joy, or resources. Also, most probably there was little in this world that was more important to Lucy and Philemon Bryan than their two sons, Reed and Tom.

A reflection of this priority is the importance the family placed on education for the boys. Information is scant, but Stetson University archives confirm that fourteen-year-old Reed attended the Academy (upper grammar school) as a boarding student for the 1890/91 school year. Reed was back again in the fall of 1893 taking a college preparatory course. There is no further record at Stetson, but apparently Reed entered college elsewhere, for he finished school in December 1898. That fall Tom, at age twenty, had entered Emory College near Atlanta.

The family's determination to provide college educations for both boys was particularly noteworthy because this coincided with the difficult economic times created by the great freeze. It explains why Tom's college education was deferred while the family focused on getting Reed through, and then supported Tom. Years later Tom acknowledged that he had helped his brother through school. In return Reed paid Tom $25 a month for school expenses. Board at Emory College was $18.50 a month, laundry $2, Sigma Alpha Epsilon fraternity dues the same, leaving Tom $4.50 a month spending money, "on which he did nicely."[10] Tom graduated from Emory College in 1902.

The freeze delayed Tom's college education, but at the same time it triggered a more unusual learning experience for him. It created the circumstances that originally brought P.N. Bryan and Tom to Fort Lauderdale. In early 1895 Henry Flagler was surging to push his railroad on to Miami. To achieve rapid completion, he divided the roadbed construction into ten-mile segments to be worked on simultaneously, and he engaged Philemon Bryan to assemble and manage a large work force for the roadbed north from the New River to Pompano.

This is sometimes depicted as a charitable gesture, but it is more properly a smart business move and a win-win for both sides. Philemon was a proven good manager and had at his fingertips unemployed, experienced workers. He assembled a work force of approximately 400 which very probably included overseers and foremen that Philemon had worked with in New Smyrna. This was not a technical job. They were to build an elevated roadbed. It was basically pick and shovel work and is best referred to as the grading contract. The overall project was under railroad supervision. Bryan signed his contract with FEC superintendent MacLain in April 1895 even before final agreement had been reached between Henry Flagler and the Brickells. That agreement providing the land and rights-of-way was dated June 12, 1895. Tom Bryan was very certain that he first came to Fort Lauderdale with his father in April 1895, and some have assumed that the full crew arrived at that time. What seems more probable is that Tom and his father, possibly with FEC personnel, came into the area for inspection and familiarization at the time of signing the grading contract. They would have taken the stage line down from the Palm Beach area and stayed at Frank Stranahan's camp on the New River. We know that after signing the contract Philemon and Tom returned to New Smyrna to recruit the labor and buy supplies, so the trip with full crew would be more likely in the June or July timeframe coinciding with Flagler's obtaining the rights-of-way.[11] This would also be consistent with Tom Bryan's later observation that when they arrived in Fort Lauderdale, fellow New Smyrna refugee Ed King was already here, and Ed did not arrive until June 2, 1895.

It is a common perception that Philemon first came to Fort Lauderdale with both sons, Reed and Tom. There is not a single reference to Reed in the scraps of information detailing the grading project. Reed was presumably in school when Philemon and Tom came for the contract signing in April, and when the full crew came down in June, nineteen-year-old Reed was probably more needed in New Smyrna. Philemon would not likely have walked away from the economic mess there without leaving trusted deputies in charge, and Reed and his mother Lucy were probably the best candidates. Statements that P.N. Bryan undertook the grading project with the help of his teenage sons would still be true whether Reed was on the ground in Fort Lauderdale or New Smyrna, but Reed most probably stayed in New Smyrna.

Bringing the 400-man grading crew to the New River site was like taking an Army into virgin territory. The group had to be self-sustaining. There was nothing along the New River except for Frank Stranahan's little camp and trading post at the ferry crossing a half mile downstream. The grading crew was comparable in size to the military expeditions that were in the area during the Seminole wars, and it would be years and years before there were 400 people again at one time in Fort Lauderdale. For Philemon it must have been reminiscent of his days as a Sergeant in the Confederate army, and he had had three subsequent decades of experience marshaling work forces. It was a challenge of logistics, and Philemon knew about provisioning, supply lines, chow lines, first aid stations, pay procedures. It was shrewd of Henry Flagler to pick P. N. Bryan for this responsibility. Bryan was in effect the colonel in charge of an army of workers and running the camp that met all their needs. His seventeen-year-old son Tom was his aide-de-camp.

The journey of the grading crew to the New River provided one of Tom Bryan's favorite stories for the rest of his life. Here is a version as told to Wesley Stout for a Beachcomber column:

> "The Bryans went back to New Smyrna to recruit Negro labor and buy supplies. Back in West Palm, P. N. hired a schooner and two sloops to transport hands and supplies to New River. Making Tom supercargo (in charge of cargo) of this fleet, the father drove to Fort Lauderdale with the two mules and wagon he had brought from New Smyrna. The three boats cast off on a Monday morning via the newly dug canal (inland waterway), but there was no wind and they were there until Tuesday night making the south end of the lake. When they got no further than Linton (Delray) by Friday, Tom grew disgusted. There was a Negro aboard whom he knew had been to Miami, and the boy proposed that the two of them walk the rest of the way to Fort Lauderdale. A second Negro joined them and they were a day and two nights reaching here, sleeping out on palmetto leaf beds, the mosquitos 'not too bad.' They had one meal, grits and bacon found in the cook shack of a railroad construction camp."[11]

Tom was at the camp a week before the three vessels. When they arrived, two were unloaded and sent back for more supplies and the third was used for temporary quarters and storage until a supply depot was built. The immediate task of the crew was to clear space for tents for living quarters, and a substantial amount of land had to have been quickly cleared for their camp adjacent to the proposed rail bed. Initially the only facilities were tents.

It was "mighty rough country, just pine and palmetto thickets and swamps and sloughs," according to Tom Bryan. [12] The crew first cut paths and cleared rights-of-way, burning trees and brush in preparation for the grading and building up of the roadbed. This was strictly manual labor, picks and shovels, and wheelbarrows. The two mules were for emergency jobs only. Standard garb for the laborers was nothing but knee-length cotton shirts.

The first payday came after about a month, and this occasioned another of Tom Bryan's favorite stories. He was sent to Palm Beach to get the cash for the payroll, variously described as $600 or $800, which he carried back in a briefcase. In anticipation of this payout, a group of Palm Beach gamblers and women chartered a side-wheel steamboat to go to the New River to exploit these earnings, and Tom accepted an offer of a ride. Tom warned the captain of the perils of a sandbar at the shallow inlet to the New River, but his advice was not heeded, and the boat grounded. It was after dark, and the boat would be stuck there until a tidal change created more depth. Anxious Tom borrowed the ship's rowboat to row the rest of the way to the camp (two miles). The threat of a rainsquall prompted Tom to disrobe and stow his clothes to keep them dry. There are various versions of this story, but the more graphic one is of a naked Tom encountering a group of Indians. It was without incident, and it all ended happily as a re-clothed Tom made it to the camp. The steamboat came the next day, and Tom has said that it took less than a week for them to get most of the $800.[11]

With time the camp became more sophisticated as lumber was brought in for more substantial main structures, most likely for floors and framing for the main facilities like the dining hall.

Philemon had a commissary or company store, and his brother Gad operated a saloon on the riverbank, but they did not create fancy quarters for themselves.[13] Tom has said that he and his father lived in a floorless shack for the duration of the project.[14]

The grading job was finished in Fort Lauderdale by the end of 1895, and Tom moved to Jacksonville to work for Southern Express as a messenger. Henry Flagler could have had a hand in that. Tom has said that "Uncle Henry" visited the project from time to time and stayed at Frank Stranahan's camp.[11] Tom may have left Fort Lauderdale before Philemon, for the camp may have been slow to draw down. Philemon took time to sell off his commissary inventory, but he was gone early in 1896, for there is no evidence whatsoever that any Bryans were in Fort Lauderdale when the first train arrived in February. That is the case also for the rest of 1896, and it seems only logical that Philemon had plenty to attend to in New Smyrna as he addressed recovery from the great freeze.

The year 1896 was a turning point for Philemon and Lucy Bryan. He was fifty-two and she was forty-five. The two older girls were married and on their own. Daughter Florence was teaching in New Smyrna and probably lived at home until 1899 when she married Fred Barrett. Reed was away at school during school terms. Tom was on the road for Southern Express, though maybe home frequently. Young Constance was a teenager. It is not the point in life that one expects to be starting over, but the Bryans were being forced into change by the crippled economy in New Smyrna. Despite their extensive holdings there, the only asset the Bryan's had that was probably worth much was 4,000 head of cattle plus the security of owning a substantial home. Philemon and Tom's experience in Fort Lauderdale undoubtedly gave them a clear sense of the potential, but they also got a good taste of what life on the ground would be like. So, even if they returned to New Smyrna determined that Fort Lauderdale was the place to begin again, they faced a big challenge of how to make a reasonable transition. The family took its time, and though we have little understanding of the processes they went through, they seemed to proceed carefully and systematically. It was almost five years before the full family was resident in Fort Lauderdale. In the 1900 Federal Census Philemon appears in New Smyrna with Lucy and Tom as of June 14, and then in Fort Lauderdale with Reed as of August 11. He is listed as Farm Labor and Owner of House, free of mortgage, in New Smyrna, and Fruit Grower and Owner of Farm, free of mortgage, in Fort Lauderdale. Then, in September, construction began in Fort Lauderdale on the large frame house facing the New River that would evolve into the Bryan Hotel,[15] and it was probably 1901 before Fort Lauderdale was truly home base for the P. N. Bryan family. At that point the resident family would have been only Philemon, Lucy and nineteen-year-old Constance.

In the interim, though, the Bryans were creating a significant presence in the Fort Lauderdale area. They were accumulating land and establishing a citrus grove. Following is a sequence of items reporting Bryan family activity in the Fort Lauderdale area from 1896 to 1900:

> "(Philemon) stayed on after the grading to sell the remaining inventory of his commissary store to the few Negroes who had remained here. Before that was wound up, he and his brother (Gad) had bought land."[10] Family sources have stated that the swath of land housing the Bryan complex just west of the railroad was committed to P. N. Bryan in 1895, even though the official deeding was some years later.[16]

> "P.N. had several drainage contracts with Model Land (Flagler real estate arm) here and around Little River in 1897, and so was much in the area."[10] "Mrs. P. N. Bryan did not follow her husband here until the fall of 1897, when P.N. bought his orange grove land and built a house there."[17] "P. N. began setting out an orange grove up river. A shack was

built in which he, Mrs. Bryan and Reed lived part of the year."[10]

"The New River Grove, which was started back in 1897 as the Bryan Grove and owned by Tom M. Bryan, was sold (in 1937). . . . The old Bryan grove consists of 168 acres of land, thirty-five acres of which are grove land."[18]

Indian Inspector A. J. Duncan gave an "1897 account of a tract of forty acres of hammock (high ground) land between the north and south fork of the New River that had been occupied by Indians on April 1, 1897, but were taken possession of by a white man named Bryan while they were on a hunt, and he at present is occupying their homes and cultivating the hammocks formerly cultivated by them."[19] Then, in 1898 P. N. Bryan requested an exemption from lands to be secured for the Seminoles.

November 1898, the *Miami Metropolis* newspaper: "P.M. Bryan has 120 acres of fine land on the edge of the glades at the head of the river, with about 6 acres cleared, upon which he has 500 fine young orange trees growing. Mr. Bryan will cultivate 4½ acres of tomatoes and ½ acre beans on his land and 2 acres of tomatoes at "Old Tommie's" camp."[20]

"Finishing school in December 1898, Reed moved down to the grove permanently. They had a cow and chickens and grew much of their own food."[10]

December 1899, a reporter for the *West Palm Beach Tropical Sun* comments on people in Fort Lauderdale from Volusia County: "I met all of them except Hon.

P. N. Bryan, his place being so far distant to take in on this trip; however, I had the pleasure of hearing from him; his son, R. A. Bryan, came after the mail, and from him I learned that they had some very rich hammock on the border of the Everglades, where they intended to make a 'Volusia County orange grove,' and would set out fourteen acres in orange and grapefruit trees next year. They also have six acres of tomatoes growing nicely and will plant six more acres in a winter crop."[21]

In the context of today's topography and infrastructure, the Bryan property would be underneath elevated I-595 between the interchanges of I-95 and Highway 441, State Road 7. The view north from the freeway overlooks the South Fork of the New River, and the Bryan holdings apparently included land on both sides of the South Fork as it angled into the area from the north. This was four to five miles upriver from the railroad crossing in Fort Lauderdale, the eventual site of the Bryan family homes.

It takes time and patience to establish citrus groves. The cash crop was clearly tomatoes, a couple of crops a year, and that quickly became the predominant agricultural activity of the area. Reed's son James, looking back years later, claimed "My father made an awful lot of money farming as a teen-ager. He made $50,000, even $60,000 in a year. He had 600 acres of tomatoes."[22] This is an obvious distortion, probably in all respects, but the message is clear. Raising tomatoes was very profitable, and it is mentioned here because, despite the early Bryan focus on citrus production, the priority probably shifted fairly early to tomatoes. The groves remained sentimental favorites of Philemon and Reed, and were undoubtedly somewhat profitable, but Bryan attention was quickly shifting to other things.

The final Bryan move to Fort Lauderdale in 1900/1901 was "motivated most of all by Reed's wish to enter the fertilizer trade."[10] This observation, most certainly from Tom, has no obvious follow-on, and it may be most indicative of the family's acute awareness of a range of opportunities in the new area. There were many needs, not the least of which was a total lack of facilities for the traveling commission buyers, indispensable middlemen for moving the produce to market. There is no indication whatsoever that the Bryans moved to Fort Lauderdale to go into the hotel business, but Lucy had had years of experience accommodating boarders and lodgers, and she would need something to occupy her in new isolated surroundings. It was a modest beginning. A correspondent for the *Florida Times Union* (Jacksonville) reported in September 1900: "P. N. Bryan, formerly of New Smyrna, will build a nice 8-room dwelling near the depot. Lumber is now on the ground and work begins today. Mr. Bryan realized several thousand dollars from his farm here last season. He will ship several hundred boxes of oranges this year from his grove, which is only three year old."[15] Less than two years later another correspondent was reporting that "P. N. Bryan was increasing the capacity of his original hotel to 50 guests."[23] So, Lucy Bryan had been quickly propelled to the forefront as an unofficial hostess in the new town, and her dining table was much appreciated. "In the early days all the growers would come down river on Sunday for their mail. The Bryans never failed to invite three or four to be their guests at the hotel for Sunday dinner. Mrs. Bryan set a good table in any case, and to men baching on a truck patch it was the best and most food in the world."[24] Lucy Bryan occupied her home in 1901, and by 1902 it was being called the Bryan Hotel and had gone through a series of additions bringing it to a capacity of fifty. Nevertheless, it still constituted the family home, and Reed had a room there. The rambling structure evolved where the New River Inn now stands. This "hotel" was the only significant structure near the railroad and a much-needed hospitality center. A half-mile down river Frank Stranahan and Ed King had built a large, two-story trading post at the ferry-crossing site in late 1901/early 1902, but Stranahan had not yet established himself by the railroad.

By the end of 1902 the Bryan family had become firmly established in Fort Lauderdale on the farm, in the grove, and at the railroad crossing site, but as far as we can tell, son Tom did not participate in this activity. Tom had started working as a Southern Express messenger in early 1896 and apparently retained this job after he entered Emory College in 1898. This is indicated in the Federal Census that categorizes Tom as a Southern Express messenger in June 1900. The job probably gave Tom easy rail access to Fort Lauderdale for visits, but he apparently did not invest himself in the early start there after the railroad grading experience. Tom graduated from Emory in 1902, committed to lifetime partner, Camille, but not yet committed to a lifetime in Fort Lauderdale, according to Camille:

> "When Tom finished college he went to New York and took a course in Life Insurance. Camille and Tom made plans to live in Jacksonville. But before they were married (1904) Tom told Camille that his father expected them to come to Fort Lauderdale. 'Where's that!' exclaimed Camille. 'Somewhere in the Everglades,' explained Tom. P. N. Bryan, Tom's father, thought there would be a great future in the area and wanted them to share in its development."[25]

So what had college done for Tom Bryan? In an interview when Tom was approaching eighty he stated: "I think whatever success I've had can be traced to the advantage of a college education."[26] We know nothing about his academic course, but he was in the Sigma Alpha Epsilon fraternity, played varsity baseball, football and basketball, and was captain of the baseball team.[27] He also lived for four years in the sophistication of the metropolitan Atlanta area. What Tom was probably referring to as his advantage, though, was a broad vision of the world and institutions and technologies and what one needed to do to make things happen. From earlier examples we have seen that Tom as a teenager was seemingly fearless in sizing up a situation and taking action. This can characterize recklessness, but college gave

Tom practice in viewing things in context, noting the dangers of carelessness as well as the rewards for well-planned action. The goals of modern American society became Tom's goals, and he was probably quite certain that what was good for society was good for Tom, and vice versa. Tom was never a do-gooder for the sake of society. Whatever he did was for his own benefit, and he considered it to be right. Add to this the competitive nature of a dedicated athlete where all is fair if you play by the rules. This becomes quite a potent mix if embodied in someone who loves challenges and feels drawn to take action. Tom was unique in early Fort Lauderdale in his capacity to address things that needed to be done and at the same time feel responsible and take the initiative to make it happen. We will see examples over and over again.

So, Tom may have flirted briefly with the idea of a career in life insurance after college, but this did not play well against his father's urging him to return to Fort Lauderdale. The Bryans' early successes there provided compelling evidence of the wealth and opportunities ahead, and it is likely that Tom was fully committed to participating by 1903. Tom did most everything with gusto, and once his mind was made up, he would have plunged fully into family activities. He teamed with brother Reed, and many ensuing accounts over the next few years treat them as an entity. Their focus was on fruit/vegetable production, but there was increasing involvement in support activities. They acquired two boats or barges for moving their produce downriver to the train station. This evolved over time into a tugboat and barge service along the river and inland waterway that at one time moved steel from the railway to the Hillsboro inlet for the lighthouse.[14] Another venture, noted in a December 1903 press report, was the construction of a tramway to move produce from the fields to the river: "In cooperation with P. N. Bryan, the (Oliver) Company is constructing a tram road, which will extend from the river to Mr. Bryan's orange grove, passing through the Company's lands and about a mile of muck, and will greatly benefit other truckers besides the builders."[28]

Though day-to-day activity was dominated by agricultural pursuits, longer term planning focused on the development of the Bryan property facing the New River across from the train station. This may have been a condition for Tom's agreeing to come to Fort Lauderdale. He had to have suitable accommodation for bringing in his bride from suburban Atlanta, and the planning process was probably well underway in 1903. Almost certainly Tom took the lead on design. The project became very grand in scale and elegance, undoubtedly taking much longer than anticipated. It was more than two years after Tom's graduation from Emory that he and Camille were married, and Tom's house was still not completed until the following year.

The Bryans were working with Ed King on the overall construction project, and Ed was probably on a par with Tom when it came to being stimulated by challenges. In 1899 Ed King had pioneered the use of hollow concrete blocks manufactured on site for a lodge at the beach. The Bryan plan would draw on this technology for a three-story, masonry hotel building on the river facing the railroad. The existing frame structure would be moved west of the new hotel to serve as an annex. Adjacent to this would be two new homes for Tom and Reed, two-story, all-masonry residences facing the river. An important feature of the whole project was that it would have its own water and sewer system, hence bathrooms, and central production of acetylene gas to feed a gas lighting system. The project was precedent-setting, nothing like it for miles around, and time would show that those masonry structures were fortresses. They still exist.

A major delaying factor for the project was the process of moving the initial Bryan Hotel. The frame structure was severed into three unequal parts. The part that had been facing the river was moved west about thirty feet. It was probably then upgraded to be incorporated into the water/sewage system. The other parts were moved to the rear of the property, but the largest part was unsightly and was eventually demolished. It probably took a good part of a year before all of this was completed in 1904.[29]

While this was proceeding, significant developments were

taking place on the other side of the tracks. In 1903 the Stranahan Company was building a two-story frame store fronting on the railroad dock. The *Miami Metropolis* reported on December 4, 1903 that Mr. Frank Stranahan had "just completed a store near the depot, 32 x 75 feet, with a capacious hall above. He is the post-master and will move the office very soon to his new building, where it will be much more convenient to the patrons."[28] The same issue of the paper also noted that the Osceola Fruit and Vegetable Company would soon build a large, well-equipped packinghouse. This building was probably going up in 1904 a block up from the river behind Stranahan's store. These two fa-cilities, both bordering Brickell Avenue, became the anchoring structures for a main street and business district in early Fort Lauderdale.

Among the challenges of early Fort Lauderdale was the lim-ited opportunity for social life. The growers customarily gathered on Sunday to collect their mail, and on any Saturday night the Stranahan store would be so crowded "you couldn't stir it with a stick."[24] This had to have been of concern to the Bryans who in 1904 had two very attractive, very eligible candidates for mar-riage: twenty-two-year old Constance and twenty-eight-year-old Reed. Available sources make very little mention of Constance, suggesting she may have been away from Fort Lauderdale much of the time. A few references to Reed associate him with visiting parties from Palm Beach, and that may well have been his main point for social contacts. In any case, the Bryan family seemed to make an effort to promote social activity for their young mem-bers. In 1904 Miss Constance Bryan gave a "party for 'her numer-ous friends' at Stranahan's Hall in honor of Mrs. Edward Neegel of Louisville and Miss Mazie Cox of Jacksonville." In March 1907 "Miss Bryan was giving a barge party for her guests, Rosa May Adams of Savannah and Eloise Stewart of Atlanta, the barge towed to the beach by one of brother Reed's launches. The barge was carpeted and hung with Japanese lanterns, and fireworks were shot off. Mrs. Katherine Wheeler Hyatt tells us that barge parties were a fixture in the local social scene."[30]

This may seem like trivia, but it is a reflection of Bryan family priorities. Philemon and Lucy Bryan were dedicated to promoting the good fortunes of their children, not just economically but in every way. They did not come to Fort Lauderdale for themselves; they came to provide opportunity for their children, particularly their sons. It explains why, as they proceeded to create their riverfront estate, the precedence went to homes for the boys on the most desirable locations, and the hotel was meant to be a showplace. This project took about five years from earliest planning with Ed King to the opening of the new hotel. After the frame hotel had been disassembled and selectively reconstituted, construction of Tom Bryan's home would have started in 1904, but the most intense building activity was in the years 1905-1907. A number of other things happened during this period, so the construction activity becomes a backdrop more than a feature in the ensuing narrative.

The more interesting action was the arrival of newly-married Mrs. Tom Bryan in November 1904. Tom had married Camille Perry in her hometown of Covington, Georgia, and after a brief honeymoon, they proceeded to Fort Lauderdale to live. Camille later recalled "we arrived in the village (by train) on the twelfth of November, about ten thirty in the evening and were met at the station by my husband's sister, Mrs. Fred Barrett and husband, with a dim lantern to light our way through the narrow sandy path to the Bryan home" (hotel annex) where they were to live "for at least a year." Tom had tried to prepare Camille for the realities of Fort Lauderdale, but she "had not pictured a place quite so devoid of people." "There were only four or five cottages, one store and a few Seminole Indians here." Her "first trip was through the little path to the big store owned by Mr. Stranahan . . . located on the river front . . . with the post office in one corner." "The next day we did the same thing, the place afforded very little variety." "When we felt the need of exercise, our only walk in comfort was through a little path which led to the Stranahan home and it did seem at least two miles (actually half a mile)." [25]

As far as her husband's activities were concerned, Camille

noted that "My husband to the farm did go, bright and early every morning." "Sunday afternoons we usually went out to look over the farm, not in an automobile, but a little buckboard with a very wild horse." "I was always very much interested in our trips to the orange grove planted by my father-in-law." Tom "also planted a small grove on lots west of town located on the river." Farming "was the chief industry." "When Camille looked out on the farm . . . she wondered how anything can grow in this sand. But the sand produced surprisingly well and that is how Tom Bryan made his first money. They grew tomatoes exclusively." "Tom was a good businessman. He knew how to make money and he knew how to save it." He "finally decided to invest in some of the white sand and while I did not always express my feelings, I often wondered all to myself just what he could do with it, but as he only paid from five to twenty dollars an acre, and twenty-five dollars for lots fifty by one hundred and fifty, now located in the business section, I thought he might be able to stand the loss."[25]

We might not want to rely on Camille for the facts, but she has done a good job conveying the essence of the emerging Fort Lauderdale. It remained a barebones place for several years after she arrived. The intensity was in the fields and groves, and the payoff was apparently excellent. Wealth was being created by most anyone who could manage a tomato patch, and no small part of that was probably being plowed back into the purchase of land either for increased production or for investment. Tom Bryan was by no means the only one gambling on growth and future demand. Feeding that speculation was the promise of draining the Everglades to create an agricultural wonderland in South Florida's interior. It was a key platform objective of Napoleon Bonaparte Broward when he ran for governor of Florida in the fall of 1904. The Bryans were "strong supporters, Reed Bryan his campaign manager in this area."[31] Upon his election in November 1904, Broward proceeded quickly. "The federal government had earmarked money for drainage projects and Broward determined to use some of these funds in Florida. Plans for drainage were soon underway after Broward took office in 1905. He selected

Reed A. Bryan to supervise the construction of two dredges."[32] So, while Ed King was constructing houses for Tom and Reed Bryan on one bank of the New River, a boatyard almost directly opposite was assembling one enormous dredge and then the other. Each dredge was "180 by 42 feet, the largest south of Philadelphia."[33] The first dredge, the Everglades, was launched in April 1906 with Constance Bryan breaking a bottle of champagne. It proceeded up the South Fork of the New River to go west into the Everglades and north to Lake Okeechobee. The second dredge, the Okeechobee, was completed in October 1906 and likewise moved up the South Fork of the New River toward Lake Okeechobee.[33]

To assist in financing the dredging operations, the State offered the sale of huge tracts of yet-to-be-reclaimed land for as little as two dollars an acre. A number of large purchases were topped by Richard Bolles' acquisition of 500,000 acres in December 1908. He would mount a national marketing campaign that would give broad name recognition to Fort Lauderdale. The manpower and support for the dredging operations out of Fort Lauderdale had already drawn in new residents and new non-farming activities, and this was adding energy to the sleepy little village. The year 1908 might well be the landmark year that Fort Lauderdale moved from being a toddler to young adolescent poised for a growth spurt.

Meanwhile, the agricultural front in Fort Lauderdale was humming along. The Bryans were tireless promoters. They appear to be the organizers of a May 1906 major event, "Excursion to Ft. Lauderdale, Harvest Home Picnic and Barbecue at Seminole Park, New River." [34] Sponsors are billed as The Vegetable Growers, Commission Drummers, and Citizens of Fort Lauderdale, but the committee is made up of Hon. P. N. Bryan, Chairman of Speaking, T. M. Bryan, Floor Manager, Dancing Pavilion, and Reed A Bryan, Manager of Excursions to the Everglades and Ocean Beach. The handbill announcing this is a gem, a hand-drawn map of the area from the beach to the everglades showing vegetable growers and acreage for each in what appears to be their approximate location along the river. By far the largest number of growers and largest acreages were along the South Fork with P. N. Bryan's orange grove at the end. North of the river and North Fork in the area closest to the railroad shows the three Bryan names with forty-five acres. This is undoubtedly the farm that Camille has referred to, accessible by horse-drawn conveyance, as opposed to the grove accessible only by boat.

A year and a half later (November 1907) the *Miami Metropolis* described the productivity of this area:

"Within this township, there are probably three hundred farmers tilling from one to fifty acres of soil. Of this acreage this season, about seventy-five percent will be tomatoes, the balance being in egg plant, pepper and beans. These vegetables have proven to be the best sellers for the farmers here. The shipment of some of these vegetables has already been made, from 25 to 50 crates leaving by train every morning. February and March, the carload lots will be going to the northern markets, and then is when Ft. Lauderdale is 'strenuous.' There will be about 500 acres under cultivation this season, from which is closely estimated that there will be yielded one hundred thousand crates of tomatoes and 25,000 crates of other vegetables. There are a couple of 20 acre pineapple fields also, besides a couple of orange groves. From the one owned by P.N. and R.A. Bryan, it is estimated there will be shipped a thousand crates of oranges and 200 crates of grapefruit. This firm has already shipped about a hundred boxes of grapefruit. The farming land is half on muck land, and half on prairie, some farmers preferring one or the other. Thus, it will be seen, Fort Lauderdale will hold a prominent place in the shipping industry this winter."[35]

A big event on the personal side for the Bryan family in 1907 was the marriage of thirty-one-year-old Reed to Anna W. Baker in Baltimore. We have few details, but the *Miami Metropolis* reported in 1908 that Anna's mother and sister had visited from Delray when the couple had been married a little over a year.[7] We presume that upon marriage Reed and Anna had moved into the newly constructed house facing the New River. By that time, Tom and Camille would have been in their house next door for more than a year, and the new hotel building would have been nearing completion. Philemon and Lucy were living in the Hotel Annex, and they would continue to live there after the new hotel opened. The *Miami Metropolis* noted in November 1907 that "Mr. Bryan has built a beautiful structure, of artificial stone, three stories high and containing twenty-five fine bedrooms, fifteen feet square, well lighted and ventilated throughout. All modern conveniences will be found in the hotel, such as baths, acetylene gas plant, electric bell service, and everything for the comfort and convenience of his guests. The Bryan House will open its doors the first of the year (1908)."[35]

Another big promotional event was staged on May 5, 1908, a grand celebration attracting 300 to 400 people, the largest crowd ever seen. The main objective was an auction of house lots in Ft. Lauderdale and about 50 lots were sold. A couple of weeks before there had been a notice in Miami papers signed by founding fathers Frank Stranahan, P. N. Bryan, and Joe Farrow promising a good time for all: "Free excursion up the river in the morning, followed by auction sale and balloon ascension, then political speeches until train time, all accompanied by a band of music. We will arrange excursion rates from West Palm Beach and Miami and all intermediate points. We are going to have an entertainment costing hundreds of dollars, all free to everybody. Come by land, come by water, come by rail, by auto, by manpower, come in a balloon."[36] In effect, this event was an acknowledgement of the prosperity and marketability of Ft. Lauderdale. Special rail fares suggest that the event was sponsored by FEC Railway interests.

So, 1908 was a good year, and quite a year for the Bryan

family. Not only was the long construction project finished and new hotel open, but Camille was pregnant and Constance was preparing to get married. Tom and Camille's son Perry was born on April 17 probably in their home on the river. Constance married John Marshall Gardner on May 14 in Fort Lauderdale, and most likely that whole event was staged in and around the new hotel. It would have been a grand celebration. Further celebrating would have been occasioned by the news that Reed and Anna were expecting. These had to have been wonderful moments for Philemon and Lucy Bryan. Their family was launched, established, and carrying on. It was what they had been working for since coming to Fort Lauderdale, and their own lives had new meaning as they served the community with a quality hotel. Everyone in the family must have been feeling pretty much on top of the world until they were stunned by a double tragedy at the end of the year. In early December 1908 Anna gave birth to a stillborn son, and within a month Anna had also died, January 5, 1909. "She had become violently ill, possibly with dengue fever, late in her pregnancy, and no medical help was available."[7] Reed was devastated. Family lore says that he disappeared into the Everglades for several weeks, and when he returned he had typhoid fever. Reed sought refuge in the hotel annex with his parents, for he is listed as a member of the P. N. Bryan residence in the 1910 federal census. It is highly likely that he never lived again in the house built for him on the New River. Within a few years that house had been sold.[37]

Shared family tragedy deepens the relationships in a well-functioning family. Philemon, Lucy, Tom and Reed were already a tight unit, and 1909 likely sharpened their commitments to each other. It would be typical of this family to be focusing on the future, and the Bryans were in good position to meet the challenges ahead. Anyone of any importance who came to town had to stay at their hotel and eat at their table. Little could happen in Fort Lauderdale without the Bryans being involved in one way or another.

Some of those visitors would have been Richard Bolles and

his lieutenants. We noted before that Bolles in 1908 purchased 500,000 acres of Everglades land. He had set up a unique selling plan and advertised nationally: 12,000 tracts of land, from ten acres to 640 acres (a square-mile section); minimum cost of $240 payable over two years at $10 per month; each purchase to include a complimentary residential lot in Progresso, a local six-square-mile parcel that Bolles acquired, "all of present Fort Lauderdale between Powerline Road and the Gateway Theater, from 6th to 18th Street north."[38] As a further inducement, "the purchasers were also to have the opportunity, at a huge drawing to be held in Fort Lauderdale in March of 1911, of acquiring as much as a section instead of the minimum ten acres guaranteed by their purchases."[39] Thousands of contracts were sold.

The Bolles staff had to have been very much in evidence in Fort Lauderdale as all of this evolved. It certainly was much talked about locally, and it did not take much imagination to project the impact on Fort Lauderdale. The "downtown" area along and near Brickell Avenue was still a very sleepy place as late as 1908 with a few small buildings along a wide dirt roadway with weeds growing down the middle, but that area would be transformed into a respectable main street in the next two or three years. As early as March 1909 Frank Oliver had built a second hotel in town back from the river and a short block off Brickell Avenue. The Keystone Hotel, a masonry building of plain concrete block, was maybe a third the size of the Bryan Hotel and most certainly not as elegant, but there was plenty of demand for rooms when the commission buyers were in town. The following year work was probably in progress to convert the large packing-house on Brickell Avenue into the Osceola Hotel, and that would add life and more class to the main street. Hotel customers now included the curious and anxious investors in the Bolles project as well as various promoters hoping to benefit from this activity.

Early Fort Lauderdale residents had undoubtedly enjoyed being beyond convenient reach of local authority in Miami. They had managed very well in a cooperative and congenial way, and there was no obvious framework in Fort Lauderdale for services of any kind. Now, as they anticipated the grand finale of the Bolles project, they were faced with something they might not be able to control. This must have been a common point of discussion, and there was no one better prepared to address the issues than Philemon Bryan. Twenty years earlier, he had been part of the organizing committee for incorporating the town of New Smyrna, and he had been the first mayor. He knew what the responsibilities were for managing a community. The Bryan family itself provided the forum for discussion and strategizing. We can only guess how this evolved, but once things began to happen, they happened so quickly that there must have been a vision and a plan. They needed to establish local structures to support a stand-alone community.

A beginning step in that direction was to establish a bank. Tom Bryan took the initiative. He organized the Fort Lauderdale State Bank, the town's first bank, though he was not an officer.

"He organized it against the firm opposition of Frank Stranahan, who was doing a general banking business in his store without benefit of a charter, and discounting his store bills with the deposits of his customers. The original capital was $15,000. Tom had $7,500 made in tomatoes. He sold $1,000 interests to Jim Gilman of the Bank of Bay Biscayne, Ed Romph of Miami's First National and his brother-in-law, Fred Barrett. The money was not payable, however, until he could issue stock, while the stock could not be issued until $15,000 had been paid into the state comptroller's office. Frank Oliver had had a bonanza tomato crop the previous season, clearing $18,000. Bryan proposed that Oliver put up the other $7,500, Bryan to repay him as he sold the stock. 'On one condition,' said Oliver. 'If you make me president. I've always wanted to be a bank president. I don't know a thing about running a bank, don't want to have a thing

to do with it, but just have the title.' And so Frank
Oliver became the first president of our first bank,
C. D. Kittredge as cashier and H. G. Wheeler as
vice-president. Stranahan changed his mind later,
bought stock and became a director." [40]

The State granted the charter for the bank on September 10, 1910,
and the bank opened on the first business day after January 1,
1911 in a small building on Brickell Avenue near Stranahan's
store.

   A next step was to get organized for incorporation as a town.
In early December 1910 a Commercial Club was established with
Reed Bryan as president, Will Marshall, secretary, J. N. Oliver
(Frank Oliver's brother), vice president, Frank Stranahan, trea-
surer. "The first session of record was held December 16, at which
time the name Board of Trade was adopted. Reed A. Bryan, who
had been appointed president at an earlier organizational meeting, presided." Then, at a meeting on January 6, 1911 two important motions were passed: a motion "that all energetic ladies
of the town be asked to meet with the board to form a civic
organization" (the formation of the Women's Civic Improvement
Association was announced at the next meeting); and a motion to
incorporate Fort Lauderdale as a town. The motions passed unan-
imously. "W. H. Marshall, Stranahan, Wheeler, and Billingsley
were appointed to 'investigate and prepare and push completion
of a plan of charter'." Billingsley, who was Bolles' attorney and
the only attorney in town, was "empowered to draw the papers
necessary under the general laws of the state." What ensued was
apparently an intense round of private discussions within the
community prompting at least one complaint about "all these
secret meetings." The record is not clear, but there is some possibility that these off-line meetings may have yielded general
agreement on a slate of city officers who actually had their first
official meeting prior to the mass meeting that elected officers,
voted to incorporate, and set the town limits at one and a half
miles square. That meeting "was attended by forty-five of the

fifty men who had been adjudged to be qualified voters." The elected officers were: W. H. Marshall, mayor; Ed T. King, president of council; and four councilmen—Tom Bryan, W. C. Kyle, W. H. Covington, and W. O. Berryhill. As first orders of business on April 3, 1911 the council hired a town marshall and addressed the issue of a mule and wagon to perform "much needed sanitary duties" (emptying privies and disposing of refuse). The state legislature approved the proposed town charter on June 2, 1911.[41]

It is clear that the Bolles' organization was working closely with the new officials. Among other things, the expansion of the city to one and a half miles square brought Progresso into Fort Lauderdale city limits. And even though the new town structure was a bit after the fact for the climax of Bolles' sales campaign, the event seemed to have been accomplished without major problems. It could not have happened thus without a lot of good organization and coordination. One observer reported: "On March 19th I saw three long, heavily loaded trains arrive. They simply filled the woods, as there was not house room here for one fourth. More than a thousand tents were put up in the piney woods between March 15th and 20th. Two years ago, Ft. Lauderdale had nearly 150 inhabitants, counting men, women, children and dogs. The town had 5,000 by March 20th; I was on the ground and counted."[42] There is not much detail about the proceedings. Activities apparently extended from about March 15 to April 1, and in addition to the big drawing there was a series of auctions. There are no reports of aftermath, so presumably most people just came and left, but some stayed and later became important players on the local scene. This event, of course, was intended to be the prelude for great things to come. So, though most of the attendees may have left, the experience for the locals was a glimpse of the reality of a much larger Fort Lauderdale, and this spurred the development that was already taking place.

Once the town government was functioning, Councilman Tom became the dominant face of the Bryan presence in Fort Lauderdale. We find little reference to any public involvement by Philemon other than the hotel, and there is not much reference to

Reed's activities. A happy turn of events for the family started in 1912 when a Miss "Stella" Ummell came to Fort Lauderdale from Ohio to teach school. A long courtship ended with the wedding of thirty-eight-year-old Reed and twenty-six-year-old Stella in Ohio in August 1914. When the couple arrived in Fort Lauderdale a month later, the *Miami Metropolis* noted: "Reed looks ten years younger and wears a smile no practiced cake-walker can equal."[7] So as Tom proceeded to a series of notable civic actions, the P. N. Bryan family base was finding new satisfaction in its Fort Lauderdale setting. Reed was undoubtedly managing the agricultural assets, while Philemon and Lucy were busy with their hotel, but by no means were they going their separate ways. One of Reed's sons in later years said that the family created a development company, so even though they all had their separate revenue streams, they were acting in concert probably much more than anyone knows.[22] No doubt the family also remained the under-pinning of Tom Bryan's confidence. He was so confident, so right. He was not a dreamer, nor for that matter a visionary. As Tom moved forward, it was just a matter of common sense. He was committed to bringing Fort Lauderdale up to standard, and he had been around enough to know what was standard in much of America. Fort Lauderdale should have its own bank, should have electricity, should have phones, should have a road to the beach, and should govern itself. Also, the surrounding dominant agricultural economy should have its own identity and representation with Fort Lauderdale as the logical county seat. It was just good sense.

Tom was not a solo act. He rarely moved out on his own in addressing any challenge. What distinguished Tom from his peers is that he was not reluctant to step in and take over when the going got rough. Consequently Tom gets credit for bold action on some things, while his role might be somewhat invisible in other actions. The first bank, mentioned previously, is a good example of Tom as the instigator with no obvious role in the final product. Without a doubt Tom was an instigator in much of what happened in early Fort Lauderdale in his role as a councilman and otherwise. The council, initially, was not perceived as an instrument for action. There were no funds to speak of. But during that first year of 1911 the council addressed proposals for franchises for private entities to establish phone service and build an ice/electric plant. The *Florida Times-Union* (Jacksonville) reported in December 1911 that "the telephone franchise, which passed city council at November's first meeting, was returned unsigned by Mayor Marshall as too sweeping and lacking safeguards of the public interest." [43] A couple of days earlier the same newspaper reported that the new ice plant was about to make ice. We have few details, and these services did not become operational until some time later. Meanwhile council attention in early 1912 was likely dominated by the preparations for the opening of the North New River Canal to Lake Okeechobee. The ceremony took place on the riverfront at the foot of Brickell Avenue on April 26, 1912 with Mayor Marshall presenting a gold shovel to Governor Gilchrist. All of Fort Lauderdale turned out. Then, little more than a month later, a huge fire at the same location wiped out the town's two big stores, Stranahan's and Wheeler's, and much of the business center. There was no fire department. The town council sprang into action as townsfolk demanded a fire department and city water and sewers. A forty thousand dollar bond issue was approved providing for a fire department and equipment, a water plant, and some streets. Fort Lauderdale was beginning to function as a city.

Phone service in Fort Lauderdale was slow to start. One source states June 1912, another states early 1914. Some of the difference may be a distinction between installing a switchboard and a full functioning service. The switchboard was installed in a private dwelling by a Mr. Wethstein, who owned a string of exchanges in central Florida. Some sources have assumed that Tom Bryan had an interest in the phone system from the beginning, which would not be surprising, but what we can verify is that Tom and his brother-in-law Fred Barrett bought the telephone system from Wethstein and a Mrs. Goodrich in 1918. They may have been partners prior to that. Tom moved the company into larger quarters where it remained until sold to Southern Bell. Tom is generally credited with establishing Fort Lauderdale's phone system.[44]

He is also credited with bringing electricity to the new town. We have better insight into that project from Tom Bryan's own account. First, it must be recognized that the commercial imperative for an electric plant was to make ice, critical for refrigerating the rail shipments of produce to the north. For years Miami had been regularly sending boxcar loads of ice to Fort Lauderdale, so that demand was guaranteed, and excess electricity could be sold to the city. The first step toward electricity, then, was an ice plant, and Tom Bryan partnered with Mr. Wheeler, Mr. Stranahan and Mr. Barrett in this venture. Anticipated production was noted in a December 1911 news account. It did not go well. A gasoline engine ran a compressor that produced the ice, but the quality of the ice using fresh water was yellow and muddy in appearance. "Disappointment in the venture raised many objections and Tom Bryan bought out the partners." He brought in an adviser from General Electric, "bought a 50 kilo generator to care for the lights in the streets and the homes," "applied a direct connecting steam engine to drive the generator," and obtained a thirty-year franchise from the city to operate. In September 1912 Tom obtained the permit from the council for the Fort Lauderdale Light and Ice Company. "Street lights were installed and Fort Lauderdale had its first electric system. A 15-ton ice plant began operating at about the same time." When Tom later began to upgrade with a bigger building and more powerful equipment, he was bought out by what is now Florida Power and Light, and they took over the expansion.[45]

The ice/power plant was at the northern edge of town west of the railroad and that street was the only railroad crossing for vehicles in the town. The FEC had refused the council's request for another vehicle crossing at 2nd St., so Tom Bryan took action. It is a great little anecdote so illustrative of Tom's character and capacity to get things done. Town council minutes of Monday October 27, 1913: "At an informal meeting of the council held in the postoffice lobby this evening, Tom. M. Bryan introduced a resolution: Whereas: the Town Council has exhausted every re-source in trying to get the FEC to install a crossing at No. Third St. (now 2nd St.), and Whereas: said crossing is badly needed by our people residing west of the tracks, Therefore Be It Resolved by the Town Council of Fort Lauderdale that the street commissioner be authorized to open such a crossing." At midnight that night, "after the night passenger train had gone north, most of the able-bodied males here, including the town officers, gathered at the railroad with picks, sledges and shovels." "In anticipation, two cars of crushed stone had been ordered and shunted onto the depot siding. The rock was transferred by wagon to the track. Timbers were laid between the rails and the rock tamped between them. About 3 a.m., amidst much whooping and hollering, H. E. Fine drove his car across. The deed was done." Before noon the next day a section gang was tearing out the crossing and replacing barriers. However, before long an FEC attorney "met with the council and agreed to the new crossing, subject to certain unspecified concessions by the city."[46]

An earlier call to action at another council meeting concerned the condition of the riverbanks. "The great fire of 1912 had left the city fathers acutely fire-hazard conscious. The riverbanks were littered with such hazards and the city had ordered all moved beyond the fire limits. H. G. Wheeler had refused to move his boathouse at the foot of Brickell. 'Let's tear it down then' proposed the direct-action Bryan to his fellow councilmen, Ed King and Deacon Berryhill. They agreeing, Bryan told Karl Goodbread (town marshal) to be on hand with a gang of men Monday morning. With Wheeler watching from across the way, Goodbread's men took the boathouse apart and stacked the timbers neatly amidst the ruins of the original Wheeler Building, where the 1912 fire had started."[47]

The condition of the riverfront was emerging as a major issue. Tearing down unsightly structures became an objective for more than fire hazards. The opening of the Everglades canal had created a new industry in Fort Lauderdale, fish-packing shacks along the river to process fish from Lake Okeechobee for rail shipment.

Quite apart from the appearance, they were smelly and polluted the river with all their waste matter. Mary Brickell, who still owned much of the riverfront, was selling or leasing to fishhouse operators "strips of land of indeterminate width between the city streets and the river with full riparian (waterfront) rights."[48] The council appointed a town attorney in December 1913 who concluded that Mary Brickell did not actually own those rights. With his urging, the Council agreed to sue. It took until 1918 to get through the appeals, but the ultimate decision was in favor of the city, and it set the framework for the wonderful public riverfront we enjoy today. It was a daring move by a fledgling first council. There is no indication that Tom Bryan played any special role in this, but he was so dominant in that body that it is unlikely the action would have been taken without his full support.

Tom Bryan was not the only big thinker in that first town government, and they were no shrinking violets. They looked at Fort Lauderdale in its fullest context, and they identified as objectives two of the most intimidating projects: a commercial port with easy access to the sea; and a roadway to the beach through a mile of mangrove swamp and over the inland waterway. Both of these issues were beyond the authority of the town, so action groups evolved as private entities with a mix of council members and prominent business leaders.

The Deep Water Harbor Company was incorporated in 1913 with fifteen named incorporators including Mayor William Marshall, Council President Ed King, Councilmen Bryan, Berryhill and Kyle, and ten others. William Marshall was elected president. The organization had a lively correspondence with the U. S. Corps of Engineers, and "plans for the harbor were essentially complete as to the location and the facilities to be included,"[49] when serious disagreement arose within the corporation. The company faded from view, but one of the realities they faced was the difficulty of getting county support for creating another port in Dade County to compete with Miami.

A similar approach by several of the same players was used with more success to build the road to the beach. "Work was begun on the boulevard to the beach in early December 1914. A stock company, composed of Tom Bryan, Frank Stranahan, Dave Oliver, W. C. Kyle, Frank Bryan, and Fred Barrett, was organized to build the bridge."[50] Plans were put on hold, however, until a new county could be formed.

Fort Lauderdale town officials had taken office knowing that a separate "Everglades" county between Palm Beach and Miami was a top priority. The agricultural area surrounding Fort Lauderdale was a distinct economy, and a separate county made sense. It was an easy sell to legislators in Tallahassee, and local officials apparently had no difficulty in getting sponsorship for the necessary legislation at the next legislative session in 1913. On May 9 Mayor Marshall, Councilman Berryhill, Reed Bryan and the local newspaper editor went to Tallahassee to promote the necessary legislation. What they got, rather than a county, was a painful lesson in politics. A bill was passed with a revised northern boundary at what is now Oakland Park Blvd, thus excluding Pompano. The legislation required a favorable vote in each of three districts—Fort Lauderdale, Dania and Hallandale—in order for the bill to become law. The vote in July in the other two districts was not even close, so the effort was defeated and could not be re-visited for another two years.[51]

A good first step in changing Miami resistance to a new county came in October 1913 in a Dade County prohibition referendum. The voting in the northern portion of the county (Fort Lauderdale, Dania, and Hallandale) forced a switch from "wet" to "dry", much to the distress of Miami residents. It appears that Ft. Lauderdale had quickly tooled up for the next political round to form a new county. Two weeks before the prohibition referendum the Board of Trade sprang into action, rallying the "dry" vote.

The campaign to form a new county never lost momentum after that. It was classic Tom Bryan in action. As when he started the bank or opened the railroad crossing, he planned, he orchestrated, he wheedled, he rallied the forces, at the same time keeping a low personal profile. This was not a crusade. This was a management job, and to achieve his goal he had to create the second significant power structure in the new town.

The Board of Trade had served as a temporary vehicle for the community to decide to incorporate and elect officials. Authority provided by incorporation was bestowed on recognized leaders, and the Board of Trade faded from view. Annual council elections, however, quickly removed original leaders in a constant re-shuffling. By October 1913 William Marshall was no longer mayor, and Tom Bryan was off the town council in April 1914. The movers and shapers needed a new base to work from, hence a re-vitalized Board of Trade.

Tom Bryan was nominally Board of Trade President. In mid-October 1913 he called a re-organizing meeting that ultimately changed this body into an elaborate organization with newly-elected officers, directors and sixteen committees. Tom Bryan and William Marshall were among the directors. One of the committees was the County Division committee. The Board of Trade became the driving force to form the new county in the legislative session in 1915.

The *Fort Lauderdale Sentinel* reported on January 8, 1915 that "an important meeting was held between the directors of the Board of Trade and Frank A. Bryan, who is chairman of the (Board of Trade's) County Division Committee. The business contracted has been kept subrosa, but Mr. Bryan, who was in Miami this morning acting in his capacity as chairman of the Board of (Dade) County Commissioners, admitted that the report is true. It is understood that many conferences on the subject have been recently held."[52]

As mentioned earlier in this narrative, Frank A. Bryan was a half-brother of P.N. Bryan. Frank was just a little older than Tom and Reed, but there is no evidence that they regarded each other as close family. Frank came into the Fort Lauderdale area about 1896/97 with members of his mother's side of the family and proceeded on to the Miami area for a few years before returning to Fort Lauderdale. In the interim Frank apparently established the ties that led to his involvement with the Dade

County government structure, and by 1911 he was chairman of the Board of County Commissioners of Dade County, though living in Fort Lauderdale.[7] Tom Bryan and Frank Bryan worked closely together in establishing Broward County. The "many conferences" mentioned in the newspaper report cited above indicate there was definitely a plan and a strategy. They must have given attention to the grassroots in the various areas of the proposed county, for there was no effective resistance from this quarter unlike the 1913 experience. Miami resistance had been softened by the prohibition vote, so the bigger challenge was the Palm Beach County portion. Fort Lauderdale was going for a much more substantial portion of Palm Beach County than provided in the 1913 legislation. The subrosa nature of pre-meetings probably related to the new county's northern boundary among other things. The optimum Fort Lauderdale hoped for was a very ambitious goal, a northern border defined by the Hillsboro canal from the ocean north of Deerfield to Lake Okeechobee. This would have given the new county access to the southern shore of the lake. Here is Tom Bryan's explanation of how the negotiations proceeded:

"(Tom) said to Frank: 'You know R. E. McDonald (representative from Dade, who lived at Fulford). Why don't we go down and ask his support for a new county?' They did and found McDonald agreeable. Now they said to him: 'You are a good friend of John Watson (senator representing Dade and Palm Beach counties). Why don't we three go see Watson and ask his support?' They did and found Watson agreeable. There was a third key man, M. D. Carmichael, representative from Palm Beach County, whom neither Bryan knew. But Tom knew Kip Reese, president of the Farmers Bank of West Palm, and that Carmichael was a director of that bank. Tom phoned Reese and asked him to intercede. Carmichael agreed to meet Tom. While not as cordial to the idea as were the Dade men, he agreed to go along if they did. The Bryans now called a mass meeting at Dania. Tom spoke, saying: 'If you will pay our expenses, Frank and I will go to Tallahassee and we believe we will come back with your Broward County.' 'How much?' asked someone. Tom thought $300 would cover it, and the meeting voted unanimously to guarantee this."

"As the Bryans left the train at Tallahassee, a telegram was handed Frank telling him of the death of a sister at Ft. Lauderdale. He had to return, but Tom went to work. McDonald and Watson were standing without hitching, but Carmichael was lukewarm at best. 'How much do you want?' he asked. 'Dade is giving us from a line below Hallandale to Pompano,' said Bryan. 'We hope you will give us from there to the Hillsboro Canal at Deerfield. Palm Beach County can't hope to keep all that long seafront much longer. If you give us the south end now, you won't be bothered further. If you don't, you're bound to lose both ends eventually.' 'From Deerfield canal due west to Lee County?' asked Carmichael. 'No,' said Bryan, 'we'd like to have the county line follow the canal to the lake at Chosen (just west of Belle Glade), making a natural boundary. And when you come to bridge the canal, Broward County will pay half the cost.' Carmichael balked flatly. Tom pulled every string. He got George Butler, a retired civil engineer who owned land at Pompano and now was clerk of the court at Tallahassee, to work on Carmichael. When that failed, he appealed to Gov. Park Trammell. That, too, failed. Tom pleaded and argued for three weeks. Frank had not returned because he did not know Carmichael. With the legislature nearing

its end and Carmichael certain to block the bill
he wanted, Tom phoned Col. Robert J. Reed, president of our Chamber of Commerce (Board of
Trade). 'I can't get what we want,' Tom told him.
'I can get a new county with the north line at
Deerfield and due west. What shall I do?' 'Better
call Bill Kyle and consult him.' The answer came
back: 'Take it!'"[53]

Fort Lauderdale Sentinel, Friday, April 23, 1915: "**BROWARD
COUNTY IS ASSURED, Bill passed House Yesterday and Will
Pass Senate Today Without Opposition**"
This must have been a highly emotional moment for Tom
Bryan. It was twenty years almost to the day since he and his
father had arrived in raw Fort Lauderdale and stayed at Frank
Stranahan's camp while they checked out the setting for grading
the railroad bed. Tom had had his hands on most everything
since: working on the farm and in the grove; navigating the river;
gathering beach sand for concrete blocks and building a house
and hotel; establishing the town and acting on issues. He was
certainly reflecting on these things as he took the train back to
Fort Lauderdale. He assumed others were sharing his joy and
satisfaction, and he expected to face a celebratory group when he
arrived. Only his brother Reed met the train. It was a bit of cold
water in the face for Tom and a disappointment he never forgot.[27]
He coped well with reality, but it dampened any enthusiasm he
had for public service, and he declined to take any role in the new
county structure.

However, Tom returned to a project started earlier: the road
to the beach. "One of the first acts of the new county was to
pass a bond issue to fund roads and bridges at Fort Lauderdale,
Deerfield, Pompano, Dania, Hallandale, and Davie."[54] That
cleared the way for earlier plans to be implemented. The contract for building the road across the swamp went to Bryan and
Snyder. S. P. Snyder worked with Tom Bryan in October 1913,
providing the rock and haulage for the railroad crossing incident

described earlier. How long they had been teamed as road con-
tractors is uncertain, but the roadway across the swamp had to
have been the most daunting of projects, and it would take a Tom
Bryan to accept the risks. The first step was the dredging of a
canal parallel to the proposed roadway with the dredging spoil
used to build up the roadbed. Bryan and Snyder put eight inches
of beach sand atop the muck dug out of the parallel canal, then
eight inches of rock. Mules, used to haul rock and fill and pull
the graders, were forced to wear muck-shoes on the job. When the
grading was completed, the surface was oiled. This was not the
broad boulevard that we see today. "It was a narrow two-car fill
without planting."[55] The roadway, the bridge, and a 1,000 ft. long
wooden-trestle causeway (the latter two under separate contract)
were essentially completed during 1916 with a grand opening
to the public in January 1917. With this, Tom Bryan withdrew
for awhile from public projects in Fort Lauderdale, though he
built roads in other areas and was very visible in the commercial
and residential real estate field. We will come back to this later,
after we note what had been happening more generally with the
P. N. Bryan family.

When Broward County was formed, Philemon and Lucy had
already moved into their new home just north of the hotel, a masonry structure built in the summer of 1914 by Ed King.[56] This
nice-size home was very much in scale with the homes built for
Tom and Reed and with similar materials and lines. The Bryan
campus was complete, though Reed's home next to Tom's may
have already been sold to the Ewings. Reed and Stella had established a home for their new family on the opposite side of
Andrews Avenue from the hotel. By the time the county was
formed Stella was expecting the first of two sons born in 1915
and 1917. By all reports that family enjoyed a low-profile life. One
of the sons later characterized Reed's activities as follows: "his
father grew to like farming because he was very successful with
it from the time he first came to the area. Even when he did not
need to farm, Reed farmed as a hobby and had a large agricultural operation because he liked to see things grow. A foreman

ran the farm, however, because Reed was also deeply involved in real estate most of his later years."[7]

It is not clear how long the elder Bryans remained involved with the New River Hotel. The Bryan's oldest daughter Virginia managed the hotel "for some years" before Philemon's death in 1925, according to Virginia's son, but the elder Bryans were still probably very much on site after they moved into their new house. Reed's youngest son remembered his grandmother as a "really good-natured southern woman always in the kitchen of the old New River (Hotel), or out back in her own kitchen taking care of the needs of her large family."[7] The Bryans probably took great delight in their three grandsons living close by during their last ten years, 1914-1924. At the end of that period, Perry Bryan, Tom's son, would have been sixteen; Reed's boys would have been seven and nine. Lucy Bryan broke her hip in 1924 and died shortly thereafter. Philemon died less than a year later at the age of eighty. The following year, Tom Bryan and family moved to a larger home facing the New River farther downstream, so the initial cluster of the P.N. Bryan family was gone from its traditional spot after 25 years of tenancy.

The family, though, still maintained its interest in the New River Hotel. After Philemon's death it was managed for a short time by daughter Florence (Mrs. Fred Barrett). Then it went through a period of hired managers or lessees, until it was taken over by daughter Virginia around 1943/44. Virginia closed the dining room and changed the name from New River Hotel to New River Inn. After Virginia died in 1948, her son Stuart obtained full ownership by buying Tom Bryan's interest, and Stuart ran the New River Inn until it was sold to the city in 1955.[57]

The New River Hotel/Inn was always stately and elegant, but it lost its status as the leading hotel in town rather quickly. The re-building along Brickell Avenue after the 1912 fire included a new hotel with private baths, the Gilbert Hotel. Then in 1920 came the much heralded tourist hotel, the Broward Hotel. So, even in the elder Bryans' last years the New River Hotel was catering to a niche market of older clientele interested in charm and quiet. It maintained a loyal following of returnees to the very end.

Though other family members were fading from view as of 1915, this is definitely not the case for Tom Bryan. He may have drawn back from public service, but he was very much in the middle of things as a businessman and developer. The origins for this go back to Tom's early real estate activities. Here are a few glimpses into how he got started:

> 1906 – Tom replaced his brother Reed as the local agent for the Model Land Company, the railroad's real estate arm. He received 20% commission on land sales. "Whenever Tom sold a piece of land for Model, he bought a lot with his commission, until he owned 700 lots, much the largest individual land owner here."[40]

> 1907 – "Mr. Craig has purchased two lots from Tom M. Bryan, land agent for the F.E.C. Railway Co. on the south side of the river." "Mr. C. E. Hedgecock, formerly of Jacksonville, has purchased from Mr. Tom Bryan, the two lots adjoining those of Mr. Craig.[35]

> 1911 – "Thirteen acres on the river west of SW 7th St. cost him $50 an acre. This he platted as Seminole Point, auctioning the lots during the Progresso lottery of March, 1911. They sold readily at $300 to $350."[40]

> 1919 – "AUCTION! On Friday and Saturday (March 21st and 22nd) at 4 p.m. each day I will offer at auction the beautiful residence lots, about 32 in number, owned by Mr. Tom Bryan, and located just about 5 minutes' walk due west of the center of town."[58]

Tom Bryan also built buildings. Still standing and still attractive is the two-story Bryan Building on the corner of Brickell Avenue and West Las Olas Boulevard, one block west of Andrews Avenue. This building, in the National Register, is "one of the first commercial buildings to be built after the 1912 fire that destroyed much of the original city. This masonry vernacular building has a brick façade which is unusual for South Florida." "It is considered the least altered building of its era in downtown Fort Lauderdale." "The building housed the post office on the first floor from 1914 to 1925 and the Fort Lauderdale Bank until at least 1924."[59] Tom Bryan also owned a "building on Andrews Avenue opposite Wall Street, long the headquarters of the Western Union Telegraph Company; and the Bryan Arcade, at the corner of Andrews Avenue and SW Second Street, which housed the Railway Express Company, for years."[27]

This may give the impression that Tom Bryan was an accumulator of assets, but he was a trader, so he was always highly fluid and diversified. Though he may have lost millions of dollars when the South Florida Boom turned to Bust in the 1920s, he landed on his feet unlike a number of his peers who totally collapsed. The Boom was fed by rampant real estate speculation throughout South Florida. This spurred enormous growth that ultimately became a House of Cards. Tom Bryan was in the middle of that frenzy and has given this illustration of how things collapsed:

> "'If you weren't here in the boom, you can't realize the utter confusion of the records when properties were changing hands three, four and five times a month, never for cash. A valid abstract wasn't quickly had then. We all believed that when I sold you a piece of mortgaged property, you assumed the debt and I could forget about it. Our lawyers told us so, but the lawyers were wrong. That mistake ruined a lot of us.'

And Mr. Bryan cited an example by illustration. He had bought Burnham's Point from Captain Vreeland for $50,000, paying $10,000 down and giving four notes for $10,000 due one year apart. W. C. Kyle asked (Bryan) if he wished to sell. Bryan said he would sell Kyle an undivided half interest for $55,000. Kyle agreed if Bryan would resell with him at the first good offer. Shortly, Kyle reported that Morang would buy for $140,000, paying $15,000 cash and $10,000 a month.

'I already have $740,000 of Morang's paper and I don't want more,' said Bryan, who had sold Morang the Harbor Beach acreage, 'but if I get $15,000 cash, it's a deal.' Morang made one monthly payment before he failed. Kyle and his bank failed in another year. Two years more passed and Bryan got a call from Vreeland's lawyers. 'How about his $40,000 of notes?' they asked. Bryan said he owned nothing; that first he had sold a half interest in land and debt to Kyle and then both had sold to Morang, who assumed all prior debt. 'True,' said the lawyers, 'but Morang is broke, Kyle is broke and the buck is back in your hands.' Bryan and Vreeland worked out a compromise by which Bryan swapped some properties against his notes." [60]

Tom and Reed Bryan's family undertook development of the Harbor Beach properties a decade later.

After a ten-year hiatus from public office, Tom Bryan surfaced again in 1925 as one of five Commissioners in a newly adapted Commission-Manager form of Fort Lauderdale city government. The commission was the legislative body and appointed a city manager to carry out its policies. It would not be surprising if Tom Bryan had been a force in pushing for this change. It was clearly intended to be a call to action, for this new government came charging out in good Tom Bryan style. The professional city manager and city engineers surveyed needs and proposed a bond issue to cover everything. Within a year the bond issue was overwhelmingly approved by the voters. It covered sanitary sewers, water plant and extensions, sewage disposal plant, incinerator, streets, docks, bridge and causeway replacements, golf course, parks and other improvements. In the same voting, approval was also given for a $2,000,000 bond issue for the creation of a deepwater port. This was Fort Lauderdale's portion of an agreement engineered by Joseph Young, deep-pocketed developer of neighboring Hollywood. Fort Lauderdale and Hollywood each contributed $2,000,000 and Young, as a private investor, underwrote the balance up to a total cost of $6,000,000. The project called for deepening Lake Mabel to thirty-five feet and cutting a deep channel through the barrier reef to the ocean. This would become Port Everglades. Signing the agreement for Fort Lauderdale were Commissioners Tom Bryan, W. C. Kyle, the Mayor and one non-Commissioner.[61] Fort Lauderdale was finally on track to get its deepwater port. Tom Bryan's closeness to Joseph Young on this project is indicated by the fact that Tom accompanied Young to Philadelphia in September 1926 for the purpose of buying dredges.[45] This comes to attention because they were there when the big hurricane of 1926 hit Fort Lauderdale and Hollywood. That was an unfortunate blow in every respect, and an additional drag on an already stumbling economy, but it did not de-rail the port project. It proceeded to completion, with the opening of Port Everglades in February 1928.

Tom Bryan was not only championing the waterways and seaborne trade during this period, he was also pioneering air travel.

"The town's first private airplane was Tom Bryan's Curtiss Seagull for which he paid $7,500 at West Palm Beach in 1925. He took out a permit for a hangar on Las Olas causeway." "Merle Fogg had been barnstorming in Florida after the first war and then was teaching an Okeechobee businessman to fly. It was Mr. Bryan who brought our first pilot here, paying him $300 a month." "The Bryan hangar was destroyed in the 1926 hurricane, the seaplane blown across the Sound against a group of Coast Guard boats torn loose from their moorings. A Miamian paid Bryan $600 for the wreckage."[62]

This did not end Tom Bryan's flying days, though. In 1927 Tom began serving a two-year term as a Representative in the State legislature, and various sources have noted that he would fly back and forth to Tallahassee. Tom and his pilot Merle Fogg were great friends, and one of Tom's favorite stories was of a time when they were on a hunting trip and lassoed a deer from the air.[26] Merle was killed in an accident in May 1928, but his influence was strong. A year later a defunct city golf course was converted by the city into an airport and named for Merle Fogg. It would be hard to believe that Tom Bryan did not have some hand in establishing this memorial. This little airport surrounded by a lot of flat land was expanded into a Naval Air Training Center in World War II and ultimately evolved into the Fort Lauderdale-Hollywood International Airport.

Tom Bryan's attention to a deepwater port and air travel did not distract him from continuing to build roads. In 1920 Tom bought out Snyder, with whom he had partnered in building Las Olas Boulevard, and moved his operation to West Palm Beach. He then partnered with Holloway. This firm during the 1920's built Connor's Highway and State Road 25, significant connectors between the Palm Beaches and Lake Okeechobee. More importantly from a Fort Lauderdale point of view, the firm of Bryan and Holloway cleared the right of way for the Sunrise Boulevard causeway, the city's second access road to the beach. Work on the new causeway, which was sixty-five hundred feet long with two bascule bridges, began on December 29, 1938, and was formally opened to the public February 25, 1940. Bryan and his associate handled the excavation and fill work.[14] Tom Bryan had laid the groundwork for both of Fort Lauderdale's access points to the beach.

The last instance we have of direct hands-on involvement by Tom Bryan in establishing the infrastructure of Ft. Lauderdale was a venture into the air waves. In 1939 Bryan received a permit to construct a radio station, WFTL. He built and operated it for a time before selling out.[27] WFTL exists today, though based in West Palm Beach. We cannot associate Tom Bryan with public projects after this time, but he remained a very active business-man, and we can imagine that his voice, and money from time to time, contributed to the amazing growth and maturity of Fort Lauderdale in the years from 1940 to 1969.

On the personal side, Tom Bryan suffered losses that were probably much more devastating to him than his economic losses in the Bust and Depression times. His brother Reed died after a short illness in 1937. He was fifty-eight. Then in 1953, Tom lost his only child and son, Perry, who died suddenly of a heart attack. He was forty-four. Tom himself seemed indestructible, and he lived to be ninety-two. His wife Camille, though, lived for more than twelve years after, so she gets the family record for longevity of residency in Fort Lauderdale. But no one who was on the ground in Fort Lauderdale when it was absolutely raw comes even close to Tom's span of experience and involvement. He knew Ft. Lauderdale when it was nothing, and in his last years Fort Lauderdale was nationally notorious for its Spring Break activities. Much had happened in between, and Tom Bryan was so influential in giving shape to all that transpired. He was the champion shaper. Here is a re-cap of defining activities and roles that Tom Bryan had a hand in:

- —New town site and elevated railroad bed, the first major transformation of Fort Lauderdale's pristine natural environment
- —Major citrus groves and farms
- —River transport service
- —First masonry residences and first-class hotel
- —Major real estate broker
- —First bank

—Fort Lauderdale incorporation
—Councilman on the first two town councils that:
    —funded a fire department, water plant, and streets
    —brought suit against Mary Brickell for riparian rights
      along the New River
—Commercial developer in downtown Fort Lauderdale
—First electric power plant and ice plant
—Phone service
—Broward County creation
—First roadway to the beach
—First resident airplane with pilot
—Commissioner on the first city government under city
  manager form that:
    —funded major upgrades of city infrastructure
    —created Port Everglades in partnership with Hollywood
      and Joseph Young
—Broward County Representative in the State Legislature
—First airport from a defunct city golf course
—Second roadway to the beach at Sunrise Boulevard
—Radio station WFTL

In one way or another Tom Bryan was involved in so much that defined emerging Fort Lauderdale, whether governmental, civic or commercial, that it is a bit puzzling why there is not more recognition of Tom Bryan as Fort Lauderdale's most influential pioneer. No other individual record can compare. Some of the explanation is found in Tom's personality. He was not power-hungry nor a glory seeker, and he was not usually a solo act. In all of his civic and public activities he acted in the context of some kind of team, though obviously taking the lead on a number of occasions. His most notable single performance was the intense lobbying that yielded the legislation establishing Broward County, but he was empowered first by the citizenry and a Board of Trade, and he was clearly acting in their stead. At the personal level Tom Bryan was probably more respected than liked. He was too confident, too right and too successful for comfort. Tom

Bryan was not a politician. He was first and foremost a businessman, and he seemed not to worry about making friends. He was straightforward and matter-of-fact in his dealings, probably without much sentiment. He likely prided himself on being fair as in a good sports contest—play by the rules and let the chips fall where they may. In a tough situation he might well have been regarded as non-caring. Tom's personal preference in most any situation was to take action, but he was smart enough to know that effective action required organization and a logical plan. He could enlist others on the basis of his logic, and he was a trusted driver more than a leader. But Tom was not unique in any of these respects. The history of Fort Lauderdale is full of men and women like this. They came in waves over the decades, and they accomplished wonderful things. They worked together in marvelous ways, and one of the more subtle aspects of Tom Bryan's legacy is that he did not choose to dominate, despite all his advantages. He encouraged the cooperative and collegial approach to local government in this city from its earliest days. Tom helped create the system and always worked within it. So, throughout Tom Bryan's decades of involvement in the public scene in Fort Lauderdale, there were others who could have done what Tom did, but they did not. We see Tom taking the lead time and time again. He was on a personal mission to make Fort Lauderdale competitive in the modern world, and he never stopped trying. Actually, Tom was a pretty ordinary guy, liked to hunt and fish, enjoyed competitive sports, belonged to and participated in most of the community organizations you would expect for someone of his standing, and to the end worked persistently at his roll-top desk. He seemed to enjoy the recognition he received with senior standing as he eased toward being the last living settler. Nice newspaper recaps of his accomplishments were published as he turned seventy-five, eighty and ninety, and that was probably about as much reward as Tom wanted. He undoubtedly did not think of himself as an icon, but that is what he really is. Tom Bryan's whole life, not just his accomplishments, represents the essence and the realities of emerging Fort Lauderdale from its beginning to its maturity.

3

Map and Pictures

The map on the next page illustrates the broader setting of Fort Lauderdale in 1900 and identifies the areas of earliest settler activity. The background map is an official 1870 Florida state survey map probably more representative of 1900 terrain than current maps. The overlays are my own.

The pictures illustrate the evolution of a downtown Fort Lauderdale at the railroad hub from one significant building in 1903 to a substantial main street in 1915. The photographs all come from the collections of the Fort Lauderdale Historical Society and are used with their permission. The commentary and dating are my own interpretation. The research for this book has made it possible to be more precise on the dating than some earlier records.

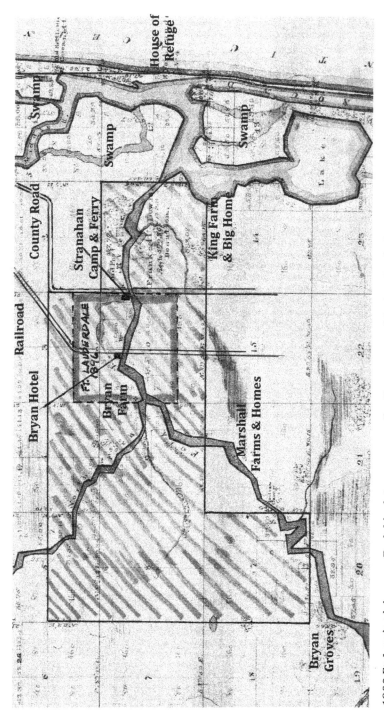

1900 Ft. Lauderdale area. Each block is a square mile. Easternmost block is Brickell "Donation" (1874); other shaded area is Brickell purchase of 1890. Ft. Lauderdale block is Flagler's plat of 1896. Relative location of early key settlers is noted.

1903. Stranahan & Co., cornerstone of Fort Lauderdale business district, first significant building at the rail hub, facing the river at Brickell Ave. Probably built by Frank Oliver, the likely dominant force in a four-way partnership. Oliver had sole control by 1911. A roving newsman visited the new store in December 1903 and reported that the post office would soon be moved there from Stranahan's trading post. Constance Bryan entertained guests in the upstairs hall in 1904, and also that year the first bridge over the New River opened at Andrews Ave., one block east. This obviated the need for Stranahan's ferry, stimulated the transition of his trading post to a residence, and generally brought focus to the rail hub as the place to go for anything. Saturday nights the Stranahan store would be so crowded "you couldn't stir it with a stick."

Ed King's Boatworks faced Stranahan's new store with a river in between. King was building barges as early as 1900, not necessarily at this site, but by 1903 he had probably begun activity here. About that time King began operating a fleet of dredges along the inland waterway. The frameworks visible in the picture to the right appear to be barges under construction.

The small structure overhanging the river at the end of the dock is the Waites family bakery built in 1904. Waites obtained riparian rights from Mary Brickell to build on the river edge. The family also purchased the boxcar that had been the original train station and used it as a residence. That is probably the boxcar seen on the left side of the picture.

On the opposite side of the tracks from the dock, the Bryan compound of hotels and homes had taken shape by the end of 1907, a precedent-setting level of sophistication: masonry structures, water and sewage systems and carbide lighting. The frame Bryan Hotel going back to 1900 became the hotel annex and was moved west. It is partially visible behind the new New River Hotel. The structures beyond are the side-by-side homes of Tom and Reed Bryan, still standing.

Brickell Ave. looking north from the riverfront in 1907/8. On the left is the back of Stranahan & Co. In the distance is the Osceola packinghouse built in 1904. In between is new construction for the Everglades Grocery. The roadbed is obviously not much traveled.

Brickell Ave. transformed in four years, looking north from the Wheeler building, probably early 1912. The packinghouse has morphed into the Osceola Hotel just beyond Everglades Grocery. New businesses line the opposite side of the street, and the roadway is hard-surfaced.

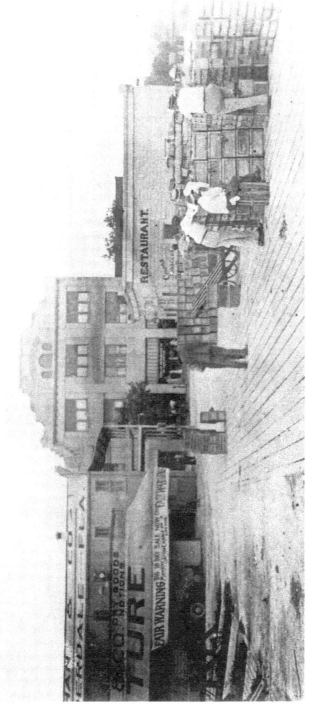

By early 1912 the new Wheeler department store had opened at the riverfront across Brickell Ave. from Stranahan's & Co. Stranahan's had greatly expended with a perpendicular addition extending from the back toward the railroad. Waites bakery had been bought out by Frank Oliver and turned over to his wife's family, Bryans not related to Tom Bryan. They replaced the frame bakery with a masonry structure that included the post office and restaurant, still overhanging the river.

Brickell Ave. from the riverfront to Wall St. (now W. Las Olas) was wiped out by fire on June 2, 1912. The fire started in Wheeler's, leaving a masonry hulk, and completely wiped out Stranahan's and other stores along Brickell. The Osceola Hotel was spared, only to burn the following year. Still, standing was the Bryan building at the water's edge. The largest structure in the distance was Frank Oliver's Keystone Hotel.

Re-built Brickell Ave. in 1915, looking south into Kings Boatworks across the river. Reconstruction achieved modernization for it coincided with first availability of city water, electricity and phone service. At the end of Brickell on the right is Oliver Bros. big store, replacing Stranahan's. Wheeler re-built across the street with a hotel that boasted the first private baths. Tom Bryan put up the building on the left right after the fire, distinctive for its red brick façade, still standing and still attractive.

4

Edwin T. King

In a contest for honors and firsts among early residents of Fort Lauderdale, Ed King would be a top contender. He was the first to buy land with the intention of farming it; he was the first to build a significant home. As Ed King gradually took on a role as a principal builder in the community, he created a notable list of first significant structures, and when the new town finally organized, E. T. King was the first Council President. He also built boats and operated dredges along the inland waterway, and at various times in his life he was a dairyman, a fruit grower and a truck gardener. So what kind of man was he? In telling about Ed King we get down to the pulse of early Fort Lauderdale

As we proceed with the narrative there will be three generations of family names. This is further complicated by a common practice of referring to men by their initials. To assist in recognition, here is a guide for quick reference to King family members and several others.

> The Family of Joseph H. King
> > Father: Joseph H., most commonly referred to as J.H. King
> > Mother: Ellen Stubbs King
> > Son: Edwin T., generally referred to as Ed or E.T. King
> > Son: Ralph

Son: Graham
Son: Richard S., referred to as Dick, Uncle Dick or R.S. King
Daughter: Margaret
Son: Dwight

The Family of Edwin T. King
Father: Edwin T., generally known as Ed or E.T. King
Mother: Susan Clifford Fox King, generally referred to in text as Susan, but she herself preferred the name Clifford
Son: Edwin Byrd, generally referred to as Bird or Byrd
Daughter: Louise
Son: Wallace
Daughter: Eleanore

The Cromartie Family
Sister: Ivy Cromartie, first schoolteacher, married Frank Stranahan, and will be referred to as either Ivy Cromartie or Ivy Stranahan, depending on the time period. Family members also in Ft. Lauderdale were:
Brother: Bloxom A. Cromartie, often referred to as B.A., married Louise King
Brother: DeWitt Cromartie

There are few pictures of Edwin T. King, but what we have indicate he was nice-looking, not distinctive in any aspect of appearance other than his ever-present moustache. He was seemingly fit, energetic and familiar with strenuous work activity, probably from the time he was a boy. He must have had an engaging and disarming personality for he made friends easily and appears to have had an easy way with any level of contact, whether millionaires or Indians. He was reasonably well educated for his time and circumstances. The 1880 census record shows Ed (about seventeen) as having attended school the previous year, and his later personal correspondence is impressive for its good penmanship, word usage and construction. He had grown up with a father skilled in building and making things, so by the time Ed was a young man he was probably already exhibiting the self-confidence and readiness to tackle anything that marked his later life. Top this with the fact that Ed came from a family steeped in southern tradition noted for respect and courtesy to others, and you have to conclude that Edwin T. King was probably a very likable and trusted guy, a very promising young man.

Ed's record indicates he was very much driven to be doing things and always intrigued by something new and different. He seemed to have good vision of possibilities and opportunities, though he was not a dreamer. He was very practical and reality-based, but he did not pull back from calculated risks that could generate something new, whether exploring new places, new techniques or new products. It was just in Ed's nature to be a change agent.

So, the Florida east coast in the 1890s was a very exciting place for Ed to be as the railroad eased its way down the coast, creating a building boom of huge, lavish hotels, opening up new markets, and creating access to new territories. Ed was in the right place at the right time and he seemed to use every opportunity to take advantage of that. This is his story from the beginning.

Edwin Thomas King was born during the Civil War on September 1, 1863[63] in Roswell, Georgia, very likely at Barrington Hall, the stately mansion of the King family. The Kings had established the town and the cotton mills that supported it. The head of the family, Barrington King, was Ed's grandfather. Ed's father, Joseph H. King, was the next to youngest of twelve children and one of three sons still living in the family home in 1860.[64] Joseph was twenty-one that year and apparently eager to get married and go to war. The marriage of Joseph H. King and Ellen Stubbs was registered on May 29, 1861 in Baldwin county Georgia. Joseph was a junior officer in the Roswell Battalion of the Georgia Cavalry, and in July 1861 he was seriously wounded in the hip, leg and hand in the First Battle of Manassas. He was discharged from the Confederate Army in 1862 and returned to Georgia and his wife and, most logically, to the only home he had known. Edwin T. King was born the following year. The year 1863 was a heady time for the Confederacy because of its battleground successes, and the King mills were humming with war production. But in May 1864 when General Sherman began his drive to Atlanta, the town of Roswell on the northeastern edge was threatened. On the night of Ed King's first birthday, the Confederate Army abandoned Atlanta, torching it as they departed. In all this process, the Roswell mill was burned, but Barrington Hall was left standing. The King family scattered, and it was probably some years before a younger Barrington King rebuilt the mills and resumed production.

The 1870 census found Joseph H. King, his wife Ellen, son Edwin T. and two younger brothers in Marietta, just a few miles from Roswell. Joseph's occupation is shown as Mnf Buggy & Wagon Materiel; his real estate is valued at $2,000; his personal estate likewise. They were not destitute. The family lived in Georgia for at least five more years (two more children were born there) before re-locating to Florida, so Ed King was at least twelve years old when he left Georgia. The only connection we find in later life is the image of Barrington Hall. That is said to have been an inspiration for the design and appearance of Ed's later construction in Ft. Lauderdale.

By the 1880 census the Joseph King family was located in Oak Hill, Florida, about a dozen miles south of New Smyrna. The children now totaled six with a year-old son born in Florida. In the occupation category, Joseph (39), Edwin T. (16) and Ralph (12) are listed as Gardeners.

Five years later in the 1885 Florida State Census Ed King at twenty-one (about twenty-two) had moved away from home and shows up as one of three boarders with the Sams family in New Smyrna. His occupation is listed as Farmer. Three residences away was the family of Dr. Fox, a town physician whose daughter, Susan Clifford Fox, was approaching fifteen. The next record we have is a copy of a marriage license for Edwin T. King and Susan C. Fox issued on November 8, 1886 in Chatham County, Georgia (Savannah).[65] They would have been sixteen and twenty-three years of age. There's probably an interesting story here, but we are not likely to ever know. What we do know is that their first child, Edwin Byrd King (later known as Bird) was born in December 1887 in Florida.

A glimpse into subsequent activities in New Smyrna comes from a page of 1889 one-liners entitled "Volusia County, Past and Present." Several entries relate to people already mentioned, or later to be mentioned in this story. J. H. King and a partner had taken over a blacksmith and wagon shop; the first lumber yard had opened, and heading the list of "those following the carpenter trade and building business" was J. H. King; "P.N. Bryan had recently built a large saw mill on the island just East of town"; the Justice of the Peace had an office in the Bryan building; Dr. Fox was one of five physicians in the county; and "E.T. King in 1889 kept a well-stocked dairy of Jersey cows."[8] (Ed King is full of surprises!)

To put this in some context, New Smyrna was incorporated as a town in 1887 with a population of 150. Philemon Bryan was the first mayor. The motivation for getting incorporated may well have been the stir created a little farther north by Henry Flagler as he built a chain of luxury hotels and in 1886/1887 began buying up railroads to facilitate the access. In the spring of 1889 Flagler's Florida East Coast Railway (FECRR) reached Daytona, only fifteen miles north of New Smyrna, and Flagler bought the newly constructed Ormond Hotel and proceeded to enlarge it. The town of New Smyrna petitioned Flagler to extend the rail line to New Smyrna to connect with an existing twenty-eight-mile standard-gauge track running in from the citrus-growing area to the west. For the next five years there was intense economic activity involving New Smyrna as Flagler proceeded south. The FECRR arrived there in November 1892 and on to Rockledge in February 1893, reaching West Palm Beach in April 1894. Concurrently, in 1893/94 Flagler was building the huge Royal Poinciana Hotel in Palm Beach, eventually the largest wooden structure in the world.

All of this must have had major impact on the King family. J.H. King, Ed's father, as a recognized carpenter and builder and part-owner of a blacksmith and wagon shop, was certainly very well-positioned to take advantage of the business opportunities offered by Flagler's activities, and we would expect that Ed King would benefit and likewise be involved. We assume that Ed and his wife Susan had lived in New Smyrna since shortly after their marriage in November 1886. After the birth of their son Bird in 1887, they had added a daughter Louise in 1889, a son Wallace in 1892, and the baby Eleanore in September 1894. In their first years of marriage they may have lived and worked on properties belonging to either J.H. King, Ed's father, or Dr. Fox, Susan's father. In any case it is unlikely that Ed and Susan were tied to any property ownership. The Fox family was probably the safe haven as Ed began working away from home, and the older children lived with the Fox family to attend school during at least one school season after the family moved to Fort Lauderdale. Ed King was most likely occupied as a farmer at least until 1890. A well-stocked dairy of Jersey cows in 1889, cited before, would not be quickly achieved nor quickly disposed of. However, a dairy requires constant attention, so Ed would have had to relinquish that responsibility before any significant involvements as a builder that would have taken him away from home. The shift from dairyman to builder would not have been a drastic transition in 1890 for someone having grown up as a farmer. Farmers expected to be self-reliant and make their own things from food to clothes to buildings. Ed King had had a lifetime of being tutored and coached in responding to whatever the needs and opportunities were, so when the demand for skilled builders surged, it was probably a logical transition for the whole King family, father and five sons of which Ed was the oldest. The best evidence of the family relationship was the teaming of Ed with his younger brother Dick, nearly eight years younger. Dick was Ed's almost constant sidekick through much of the 1890s and played a big role in the King's start-up in Ft. Lauderdale. It is also possible that Ed became spokesman for the group so his presence and representations at Flagler headquarters carried some clout and created long-term relationships that extended into the next decade.

Various scraps of information give some insight into Ed King's early involvement with the Flagler organization and its interests.

"When the FEC ended at Rockledge (February 1893), King was a contractor at New Smyrna, a friend of Flagler and his staff and often in the railroad offices at Saint Augustine. On such a visit Flagler asked him to explore the lower coast and locate the best potential deepwater port. King sailed south as far as Biscayne Bay in his own boat. When he reported back, he told Flagler that a large lagoon known as Lake Mabel (Port Everglades site) was separated from the sea by a narrow strip of land, with deepwater only 500 yards offshore. Flagler's own engineers later checked and confirmed King's findings." This is consistent with Ed King's daughters' recollection of "being told that their father and Uncle Dick King had made more than one boat trip to this area before the family moved here."[66]

In the meantime (1893/4), "King went on south to Palm Beach to help with construction of Henry Flagler's Royal Poinciana Hotel."[67] With completion of the Royal Poinciana in early 1894 and pending firm decisions about extending the railroad beyond Palm Beach, "they were marooned there for months, during which King built the Bradley brothers' casino."[68] Forty years later, Susan King reminisced: "We started in a little boat with a sail and an engine, hoping that we could get here. They were building the Breakers and the Poinciana hotels and we stayed in Palm Beach for six months."[69]

There is no doubt distortion and inaccuracy in these scraps of information, but there is a common thread that makes it highly unlikely that Ed King was a fruit grower in New Smyrna in

1895 as some accounts have surmised. On the contrary he had significant experience building some of the most sophisticated structures of his time.

Another piece of background speculation concerns Ed and Dick King's experience and interest in boating. When the King family moved from Georgia to Florida in the latter half of the 1880s, they settled in Oak Hill, a bayside community near the coast. The boys in the family must have had early contact with water activities, becoming very comfortable taking long boating explorations. They may have had early experience, with the help of their father, making their own boats. In any case, Ed King's cat-boat (single sail with a small motor) was an important instrument in introducing him to the Fort Lauderdale area and then bringing him here to settle permanently.

The final bit of speculation before focusing on the new life in Fort Lauderdale is an evaluation of Ed King's motivation. The common attribution is to the big freeze that destroyed the citrus groves in New Smyrna, but it is highly likely that Ed had made his decision before that and was only waiting for the railroad to finalize plans for southern extension so a life-line would be assured. When Ed and Dick King had explored the area in 1893/94 they certainly had long conversations with Frank Stranahan at his overnight camp on the New River, with the keeper of the House of Refuge Dennis O'Neill, and with Captain Valentine, a surveyor who resided at the House of Refuge.[70] Valentine was a friend and sometime employee of the Brickells who owned six and a half square miles of the choicest land straddling much of the New River. Valentine and O'Neill would have told Ed and Dick of a land grab in progress with investors, including themselves, buying up cheap land in anticipation of future development. Stranahan would have told how he had been enticed by the Brickells to move upstream from his original camp because the road bed had come along the high ridge line the Brickell's were protecting for later development, and Dennis O'Neill would have shown that he had purchased significant acreage that abutted Brickell's property and included the extension of the high ridge land going south. When Ed King returned for good in 1895 he immediately occupied and purchased 20 acres of this property from Dennis O'Neill for $400.[71] Preliminary agreement had most likely been reached earlier.

The lure of being a landowner and producer must have been a major factor drawing Ed and Susan King to Fort Lauderdale. Having grown up in a community where citrus grove owners were king, this was their chance to make it big. Subsequent chronology suggests that Susan may have been the more ambitious of the two while Ed was the more adventurous. In any case, the prospect of having land that would accommodate a big house that Ed would build was likely an important incentive, and there was a definite commitment to creating a citrus grove and growing crops. Five years later after Ed had gathered credits as a builder of houses and boats, he still characterized himself as Fruit Grower in the 1900 census.

The move to Fort Lauderdale began on June 2, 1895. Ed King (about thirty-two) and his younger brother Dick (twenty-four) arrived in their catboat at the Fort Lauderdale House of Refuge and stayed overnight with the new Keeper, John Fromberger.[72] Fromberger had replaced Dennis O'Neill at the end of 1894. O'Neill had been hired by Hugh Taylor Birch and his partner John MacGregor Adams to be the property manager of the 63 acres adjoining the House of Refuge to the north. Birch and Taylor had purchased that in May 1893 and had brought in a houseboat for temporary lodging.[5] So, O'Neill would have been a close neighbor of the Frombergers. Most likely the King brothers touched base immediately with O'Neill concerning the purchase of the property that would become the King farm and home.

The following day the brothers proceeded the two miles up the waterway and the New River and pitched their tents next to Frank Stranahan's camp. They undoubtedly used this as a base while they scouted their new property and developed a scenario for getting started on developing it. The challenge had to have been awesome in every respect: a new pride in ownership; a huge job of clearing and converting to arable fields; and an immediate need to establish basic housing. The site was nearly two miles from Stranahan's camp, three-quarters of the way by water down the New River to Tarpon Bend and up the Tarpon River, and the last half mile by land. The upper boundary is now SE Fourteenth Street, and the property extended east into the New River Sound. It is possible that the Kings' new property had at one time been cleared in the early 1800s by the Lewis family settlement, but in 1895 it would have had sixty years of unimpeded growth, and the high ridge ground undoubtedly had a good stand of mature trees. The King brothers started by building a "shelter of saplings cut on the site and covered with building paper and canvas brought from Palm Beach."[72] They progressed to a minimum structure that looked more like a house and proceeded to clear the land.

We have no detail of what happened on the site in the almost nine months before the railroad and King's family reached Fort Lauderdale, but we can make several assumptions. The bulk of the work was done by the King brothers, but they engaged additional help where possible. Ed King took an Indian with him when he met the train the following year. The siting for a grand house was probably an early consideration as they laid out the property, but priority was probably given to creating arable land with some initial planting of young trees and vegetable crops. Susan and the children were in Palm Beach, 45 miles north by inland waterways, and there may have been several trips to visit and get supplies. At some point Ed and Dick may have been joined by Ed's boy Bird, age seven going on eight. By some accounts Bird was already in Fort Lauderdale when the rest of the family arrived, though most accounts assume that Susan arrived with all the children.

Also, significant things were going on around them. Others were arriving. Dick King recalled years later that he had been at the Stranahan store for supplies and was returning in the dusk by boat when he found a sailboat entangled in overhanging growth. It held three men trying to find the Stranahan camp, Frank Oliver and two others on their way farther south to put in a ten-acre orange grove for a new owner.[72] Frank presumably finished that mission, but found his way back before long to Fort Lauderdale and became an important part of its story.

The biggest excitement had to have been the arrival of a 400-man construction crew in the summer of 1895 to build the railroad bed from Fort Lauderdale to Pompano. The crew was from New Smyrna and was managed by Philemon Bryan and his teenage son, Tom. The King brothers certainly knew the Bryans, and during the months of railroad-bed construction the Kings and Bryans must have become well acquainted within the small social circle that evolved around Stranahan's store and camp. They undoubtedly traded stories about the aftermath of the big freeze in New Smyrna and the trials and tribulations of pioneering in Fort Lauderdale.

The first train arrived in Fort Lauderdale on February 22, 1896, carrying Henry Flagler, Susan King and the three youngest King children, and several other passengers. The bridge and railway line south were not yet complete, so after an appropriate amount of time, the train returned backing up to West Palm Beach. Looking back in 1935, Susan King recalled her arrival: "We got into the little boat with the sail and an oar to scull with, and that was the way we travelled from the station. We landed in a hammock (high ground), now Rio Vista Isles. At the end of the path about one half mile we came to a clearing where there was a little cabin made of tarpaper roofing which was to be our home for six months until another house was finished. We lived in the new house for a year and a half, when we built our home in which we lived for twelve years. It took a long time to do things then."[69]

With the arrival of the family the priority probably shifted to building. Dick King may have taken the lead on the agricultural side as Ed planned and engineered the construction of a grand home. The house was finally occupied in 1898, assuming Susan King's timeline above is reasonably accurate. J. H. King, Ed and Dick's father, may well have assisted in the final construction. The King girls attested that "Ed and Dick's father and mother followed them here. They moved on in 1898 to Dania where the elder King had a sawmill."[17] Another brother, Ralph, followed later.

The new King home was so out of character for the area that it became something of a distinct institution. It was "a seven-room plastered house with a bathroom, quite a rarity around the turn of the century in the swamps of South Florida."[67] The King residence became the center of social activities. "The first dances and all the early entertainment were held in the second King home, built in 1898 or 1899, with its big first floor room."[73] It was the scene of weekly prayer meetings for the older residents and Sunday School for the children. Mr. and Mrs. King hosted traditional eggnog parties for the residents at Christmas and they were gala occasions.[74] The Kings provided the music, the food, and on occasion overnight lodging.

Wesley Stout found a clipping written by the local *Florida Times-Union* (Jacksonville) man at Christmas of 1899: "Quite a number of young people recently enjoyed a grand ball at the Edward King residence. Refreshments were served at intervals, the tables being loaded with delicacies. Music was furnished by the string band. It was one of the grandest social functions of the season."[75] Ivy Stranahan (the town's first schoolteacher who was living with the Kings at that time) commented on the string band, saying "There were never more than three pieces and often only one. It would be a mouth-organ, a guitar or mandolin and Charley Root's accordion. Though the King's later had the town's first piano, there was none in 1899, but they had the largest house here and were the most hospitable of folk."[75] Core musicians were probably the King brothers. According to Mrs. Frank Oliver, both Ed and Dick played musical instruments,[76] and when brother Ralph was on the scene he played a mouth-organ for dance music while dancing himself. Another mainstay was probably Charley Root and his accordion. Charley was a family friend, a fellow-refugee from New Smyrna.[17] As a general commentary, Wesley Stout noted that "like true pioneers, the hardy danced all night, the less hardy went to sleep on the floor in a corner if they could find a spot not already pre-empted by the young children of the dancers."[75]

Extraordinary measures taken by young adults to attend

King family festivities have been noted by Mrs. Frank Oliver: one young lady waved down a freight train for a ride into town; two young men spent a whole day poling a raft down the river.[76] Stout added that "Dania people (came) up over the sand road for these parties. Locals usually came by boat, up a creek that in time became the so-called Tarpon River."[75] The reality was that getting to the King residence was not convenient for anyone, including the Kings. The Tarpon River was a good third of a mile north of the house, and it was a similar distance west to the old stage road to Miami at which point it was most of a mile due north to Stranahan's and most of 5 miles south to Dania. "Ed King opened and rocked a path from his home to the Miami Road about 1896. The Kings used bicycles and the children had a pony, but if there was a package or groceries to carry they always went by boat down the Tarpon River and up the New (River)."[77]

Getting to the school site was another problem. It was west well beyond the Miami Rd. and north close to the New River. This required clearing a path through undeveloped land and over the creek-like upper reaches of the Tarpon River that at that time did not make the loop that it does now. Bird King claims he spent much of his first three years in Fort Lauderdale clearing a path from home to the school. It had to be wide enough to avoid the rattlesnakes with a footbridge over the creek[68] Ivy Cromartie Stranahan used this path when the school opened in 1899. The school's first teacher, she lived with the Kings and recalls walking a mile and half each way every day and seeing wildcats, turtles, raccoons and other creatures along the way.[78]

Ed King took the lead in establishing that new school. The Kings and the Marshalls were the first settler families to bring in children. Other settlers, though active in developing the land, were slow to move in their full families. Consequently, it was several years before the community could meet the Dade County requirement for a minimum of 10 students to open a school. The older King children returned to New Smyrna to live with their maternal grandparents for some school years, but in 1899 Ed King petitioned for an exception. The School Board agreed to provide a teacher and building materials if the community would construct the school building and come up with at least nine students. The Kings and the Marshalls provided seven, and they were able to find two more. The Fort Lauderdale public school opened on October 2, 1899.[79] By the end of that school year there were fourteen students. Ed King is credited with building Fort Lauderdale's first school, and he certainly must have organized and directed the process, but the construction was a community volunteer effort on everyone's part, and the structure went up very quickly. The school was located on Andrews Avenue on the corner of the second block south of the river.

It is difficult to keep in mind that Ed and Dick King came to Fort Lauderdale to be farmers, and they worked hard at that goal in the first years along with building a house. Some proof of their agricultural pursuits comes from an article in the *Miami Metropolis* of November 1898: "E. T. King has 25 acres located about one mile below the post office upon which he has 7 acres cleared. He has some orange trees, mangoes, pears, etc., growing. Mr. King will cultivate five acres of tomatoes. R. S. (Dick) King has 10 acres, with 3 ½ acres cleared, adjoining the above place, upon which he has oranges and a miscellaneous lot of tropical fruit trees growing. He is growing 2 ½ acres of tomatoes."[20]

As if this were not enough activity during this period, Ed King somehow started his boat-building business. It is unclear where and how this began. Boats were the indispensable accessory for doing anything in early Fort Lauderdale, so the need and the priority are clear, and it seems only logical that Ed King would establish some base on the water that would facilitate boat usage and serve as shop, storehouse, boat storage, etc. However, there was no obvious place convenient for Ed King for such a facility. His property extended through the mangrove swamp into the New River Sound, but there is no evidence whatsoever that there was any functional access there. Later pictures show a substantial King Sons Co. Boatworks on the New River where boatyards still exist by the railroad crossing, but that was so far removed from King's early activities that some interim location seems probable. A likely possibility is that King's boat business evolved out of his relationship with John MacGregor Adams who, with partner Hugh Taylor Birch, owned the beach barrier strip north of the House of Refuge. A facility fronting on the inland waterway would have been built for Adams and maintained by King. This base on the water would also be consistent with reports that the Kings frequently used the Adams' boat, the Helen B., when the Adams were gone, giving rise to the perception that the boat belonged to the Kings. Ed King most probably loved boats and being on the water, an interest he shared with his son Bird. This was reinforced while Bird was in New Smyrna with his grandfather. Dr. Fox had a pier where he had provided docking for the houseboat of a wealthy seasonal resident. Upon departure, the guest had left Dr. Fox his launch, a 2.5 horsepower, 1-cylinder gas boat, and Dr. Fox gave it to his grandson, Bird. Thus, "as a boy of twelve or so, Bird had the first power boat on the New River."[68] He was active on the water with his launch, using it for charter for $5, and also using it to tow a barge for beach-goers on Sundays. Other reference to Ed King and Bird making boats suggests that an early coaching process may have led to the robust boat business that was eventually established.

Ed King might rather have been building boats than houses, but building houses was his earliest claim to fame in Fort Lauderdale. His big home and the exposure it received as a social center could not have been a more effective showcase of Ed King's building expertise, and it made him the go-to guy for anyone interested in having a special building. By the time he had completed his own house he was probably already in discussion with John MacGregor Adams about constructing an elaborate hunting and fishing lodge on the beach property just north of the House of Refuge. Construction may have started as early as 1898, was in progress in 1899, and was essentially completed by the end of 1900, though Ed King was still working on final touches in February 1901 when Adams and guests moved in.[80]

This was major construction. A *Florida Times-Union* (Jacksonville) correspondent described the structure as being

142 feet in length and sixty-five feet wide with thirty-seven rooms of which twenty-three were on the first floor.[15] These numbers may be questionable, but there is no doubt that the structure was large. Adams was working with Chicago architects on the design in the shape of a gun, meaning a long straight barrel with a short wing at a forty-five degree angle constituting the stock. It was essentially a two-story structure with a masonry first level and frame second level, and an attic level with dormers. A particularly noteworthy feature was the use of hollow concrete block for the first level. Ed King has been credited by some as the inventor of this building material, but it was a technology just coming into vogue around the country and was probably prescribed by the architects. Together with Ed King they devised a hollow concrete block made with local beach sand that could be produced on the site. Samples were taken to Chicago three times for testing before the architects gave their approval, after which Ed King made hundreds of molds for mass production of the block.[81] It certainly set an important precedent for local building and gave Ed King one more unique skill.

Adams named this home Las Olas. Dick King claimed years later that "his brother and he built Las Olas Inn without the aid of a single experienced carpenter or mason. There were none here other than Ed himself, and he made out with any local man who was looking for work. One was Frank Oliver."[72] Another report points out, though, that "as construction began, two tar-paper shacks to house Negro craftsmen, were added."[68] A June 1901 Flagler publication described this palatial winter home as follows: "Last summer (Adams) completed one of the finest winter residences on the East Coast, costing many thousand dollars. The building is located on a high plateau of land overlooking both ocean and the sound. The lower story is constructed of made stone, the second of wood with shingled sides, and broad porches. The furnishings are elegant."[82]

The same publication also noted that "there will be several new residences built during the summer months (of 1901) in the village and on the farms lying adjacent to the town. Mr.

Frank Stranahan, the popular merchant, will erect a large and modern store building, his present quarters being inadequate to accommodate his increasing trade."[82] This report helps establish the sequencing of Ed King's activities, for Ed is the acknowledged builder of the Stranahan house. He presumably proceeded with construction during the summer or fall of 1901. The previous year Frank Stranahan had married Ivy Cromartie, the first schoolteacher, so it might be presumed that this two-story frame structure with sweeping porches was intended for their residence. However, it was built as a commercial structure replacing Stranahan's first trading post and post office at the ferry crossing.[83] Construction without amenities probably proceeded quite expeditiously. Within a couple of years, Stranahan and Company had built another new store facing the railroad dock. Subsequently, the building at the ferry crossing was converted to the Stranahan's home with appropriate amenities and became known as Stranahan House. It is considered the oldest surviving structure in Broward County.

Even before this project ended, Ed King was in discussion with Hugh Taylor Birch about building a home for Birch on the beach. A (West Palm Beach) *Tropical Sun* correspondent reported on September 20, 1901 "it was definitely assured that E. T. King will build another large cottage this winter for Mr. Burch (sic) of Chicago."[84] Birch and Adams had had a falling out, and in March 1902 they split their land near today's Poinsettia Street (a block north of Las Olas Boulevard), with Birch taking the northern portion. Birch engaged Ed King to build a two-story winter home for him around Granada St where the Westin Hotel is now located. Birch called his place Villa Moonflower. There is no information to determine if the structure was frame or masonry. Presumably the cottage was built in 1902 in anticipation of the following winter season. DeWitt Cromartie, a younger brother of Ivy Cromartie Stranahan, worked on this project as an apprentice carpenter.[85]

In contrast to the landmark construction projects built by Ed King, a small house in town is the next endeavor reported

(September 1902). Wesley Stout learned from Ed King's daughter that this was a small rental house on the north bank of the river between Andrews and S.E. First Avenue. She further pointed out that the celebrated King-Cromartie house in which she lived had been started in 1905 by the Raulersons and completed by her father.[86]

It is hard to imagine that Ed King had any time to devote to farming. Presumably Dick King had taken the lead on the agricultural side of things, but by 1901 Dick had moved to Dania to manage a grove of 1500 citrus trees, and also raise tomatoes.[82] He was not that far away and continued to work with Ed from time to time on his projects, but there could not have been much focused attention on agricultural objectives in the King household. Ed probably continued to raise a few tomatoes, but a December 1903 report on Fort Lauderdale Growers described E. T. King as a "contractor and builder and trucks as a sideline."[28] Nevertheless, the Kings had more than doubled their land holdings by 1904 with the purchase of an adjoining 30 acres.[87]

A more compelling competing interest than agriculture was the evolving boat and waterways business. Roads in the area were very slow to develop, so demand must have been high for utility barges and other watercraft. In September 1900 it was reported that "Mr. E. T. King, who has the contract to build the Adams cottage, is building a 30-ton lighter (flat-bottomed barge) to transport materials."[15] This was very likely being done at the boating facility on the Adams property fronting on the inland waterway. At that point in the Las Olas Inn construction project the need for a barge was very likely for bringing in a huge quantity of furnishings. But, when that purpose was met, what would you do with a barge? Maybe you could put a shovel on it and call it a dredge. This is highly speculative, but it is characteristic of Ed King's modus operandi. He was not a strategist. He was simply a very talented and clever man who capitalized on opportunities. In any case Ed King was likely drawn into dredging about this time through his ties to the Flagler organization, and that may have been the impetus for his establishing the King Sons Co.

Marine Ways & Boat Works, a major facility on the south bank of the New River.

Stout has noted that "As talk of the state draining the Glades grew, Flagler decided to drain his own lands to avoid a coming drainage tax,"[68] and the *Miami Metropolis* newspaper in December 1903 reported that Ed King "has been conducting the donation dredge work in Little River, New River, Cypress Creek and Hillsboro River. Mr. King looks upon this work as of great value, like so many others that have been fostered by Mr. Flagler."[28] Another undated report probably from this time period states that "Mr. E. T. King, of Fort Lauderdale, owner of the dredges and contractor of the dredging operations between Lantana and Deerfield, also J.S. Frederick, superintendent of East Coast drainage operations, were in town recently. Work is progressing rapidly. The dredge west of here has been making remarkable progress, having already completed five miles of the canal and having only about a half mile to cut yet, when there will be an open channel to a mile south of Delray, or, in all, ten miles south of Lantana. Mr. King hopes and is confident that the dredge Gaitor, west of here, will meet the dredge Wild Irishman coming up from Boca Ratone some time in November."[88] Working his way south, "Mr. King is (in Dania) with his dredge and ready to commence excavating the much talked of canal from the ocean to Dania as soon as the new dipper arrives from New York, which is expected every day," reported in the *Miami Metropolis* on July 7, 1906.[89]

But all of this did not keep Ed King from taking on another building project, likely taken on as a favor for a friend, and strengthening a continuing relationship with the Bryan family. Young Tom Bryan had graduated from college, returned to the family business, and was on the brink of getting married. What evolved was an ambitious plan to establish a distinctive family compound on the riverfront property next to the railroad. It would have an appropriate home for Tom and his bride, a corresponding home for older brother Reed, and an upscale hotel that would replace the existing hotel/boardinghouse. The group of buildings would be supported by central water and sewage systems and gas lighting system. The existing Bryan Hotel would be selectively dismantled and moved. A portion would be upgraded and serve as a hotel annex and continuing Bryan family residence.

This was certainly a very exciting challenge for Ed King, and he and the Bryan family made a very effective team. Philemon Bryan was obviously the strategist and financier, Ed King was the technical driver, Reed Bryan was a helper, and Tom Bryan probably took the lead on design and became the project manager. The chemistry between Ed King and Tom Bryan, particularly, must have been very good. Ed and Tom were both trailblazers in their own way, eager to try the latest thing and set precedents. A fundamental decision, probably from the beginning, was that the new buildings would all be masonry structures, using the hollow-block technology Ed King had perfected in building Las Olas. Those were plain blocks, but Tom would have been familiar with contoured brownstone structures, and he likely drove a decision to use commercial forms to simulate that surface for the exterior of the new buildings. We do not know how these decisions evolved, but we can imagine the excitement they generated for the King-Bryan team and other observers. The riverfront must have looked like a cement block factory for several years as all this came together.

It took five years from planning to completion of this project. An early action was probably establishing the water supply with a well and water tower. The first building-related activity would have been the dismantling and moving of the rambling Bryan hotel/residence. The structure was divided into at least three unequal sections, with a main component moved thirty feet to the west and re-positioned at the end of present-day Nugent Ave. This component was then upgraded with water supply and the beginnings of the sewage system. This had been accomplished by November 1904 when Tom's wife Camille arrived in Ft. Lauderdale. By that time, Tom's house was under construction though not available for occupancy for another year. It is likely that Reed's house next door to Tom's was built in somewhat the same time frame. Camille recalled how Tom and Reed would take a barge to the beach to get sand for the cement blocks. Tom's house was finished first in 1905, and Reed's house was probably moving along to completion when the first steps were taken in 1905 for construction of the masonry hotel. The whole cycle was essentially complete by the end of 1907, with first guests at the new hotel in early 1908.

It is hard to appreciate how distinctive this small campus of masonry buildings was in 1908. They represented an unprecedented degree of elegance and luxury in Ft. Lauderdale. In a setting where outhouses and rainwater cisterns were the norm, the Bryan site had its own water supply supported by a sixty-four-foot well and water tower, and its own sewage and irrigation systems. Thus all the Bryan structures had bathrooms. The water supply was also a critical component of the carbide lighting system. Acetylene gas was produced by water dripping on calcium carbide pellets in a separate masonry structure built away from the hotel and homes. The gas was piped from there to lighting fixtures inside the hotel and houses, creating a bright, broad light.[90]

The new buildings themselves were fortresses of contoured hollow cement block, gravity structures held together by their own weight. The severity of these lines was masked by lofty wrap-around colonial-style porches, and the metal-clad roof of the hotel was perforated by a series of dormers providing light to the third floor rooms. Solid Dade County pine, extremely hard and termite-proof, was used inside and out for the wooden supports and infrastructure. The finished structures are still impressive looking, and in their day and in this locale they were absolutely revolutionary.

Ed King must have been extremely proud of this project, probably the most satisfying he ever did, considering the total scope. Nevertheless, throughout the five-year period involved, Ed King remained otherwise engaged at times. Dredging was probably the biggest distraction. We have already noted that Ed had his own dredges operating along the inland waterway at least into mid-1906, and he almost certainly became engaged in the building of the two large dredges commissioned by the State of Florida to dredge the canals connecting with Lake Okeechobee. Gov. Broward took office in 1905 pledged to drain the Everglades, and he wasted no time in getting started. He shortly selected Reed Bryan to supervise the construction of two dredges in Ft. Lauderdale. At this point Reed and Ed King were working together on the Bryan residences, and they must have had long conversations about building dredges. It seems very probable that Ed was a consultant throughout the project, but the dredges were not assembled at his boatworks, possibly because of the limitations imposed by the railroad bridge. The dredges were built at a yard just west of the railroad bridge directly across the river from the Bryan complex. Materials were on the ground in Fort Lauderdale before the end of 1905, and the first dredge, The Everglades, was launched in April 1906, touted as the largest and finest dredge south of Philadelphia. The second dredge, The Okeechobee, was launched in October 1906. They both headed west up the South Fork of the river, and by midsummer 1907 both were cutting canals.[33]

There may be a connection between this big project and the small King house built across the New River from Stranahan's as early as 1905. When this house, subsequently known as the King-Cromartie house, was moved upriver in 1971, they found joists of huge, rough-hewn timbers of the size used for building the dredges. "Some of the joists are 12 inches by 8 inches, some are 12 by 4. They're next to the (more standard) 4 by 8—all different sizes just scrapped together."[91] If we could look behind the walls we might well find other evidence of scrapping together. It would be in character for Ed King to find productive use of leftover materials, and it was undoubtedly common pioneer practice. In any case, Ed King probably did not lay the foundations for this house, since it was Louise King Cromartie's recollection mentioned earlier that this small house was begun by the Raulersons in 1905 and finished by her father.

The origins and motivations for this little house have been

the source of some confusion and error. It was initially a one-story four-room box with no bathroom and no attached kitchen built at a time Ed King was living in and working on the most sophisticated housing in the area. Some reputable sources have stated that the family moved to this site because their large house burned in 1906. That is just not true, and the best evidence is Susan King's own word that she lived in her first large house for twelve years.[69] That larger home did eventually burn, but not until after 1910.[92] The small house started by the Raulersons was simply the King's house in town, and there was good reason for wanting a base of operations on the river site close to everything. Everyone in the King family would have applauded that convenience, but there is no way that the cottage would have sufficed for a full family move until after Ed King's major upgrades in 1911. Whatever the case, the small house was livable by 1907, and we have a record of the King's entertaining a visitor there in 1907 not long after they had moved in.[93]

With the completion of the Bryan project in early 1908, Ed King may well have turned much-needed attention to personal and family affairs. Within a decade, Ed and his wife Susan were leading separate lives, and the roots of the problem likely go back to the time period we have just discussed. Ed was so involved away from home that he could not have been giving proper attention to his farm or his home life. The burden had fallen on Susan, and while she was probably a better businessperson than Ed, she may not have been happy about it. She very likely resented being stuck out in the country while Ed was creating cutting-edge living in town for other people. What happened to the fruit groves and other farming? At least some of the farm became a quarry and the agriculture was apparently abandoned. One of Wesley Stout's anecdotes roughly dated around 1905 tells of an unusually heavy blast at the King quarry that shook the town.[94] The Kings owned the original rock pit in Ft. Lauderdale and leased it to the Hutton-Gladden Co.[95] A 1928 map shows this rock pit running from SE Twelfth Street to SE Fifteenth Street at an angle where we now have Cliff Lake, though the rock pit was much larger than the present lake. This would have taken a substantial amount of the King property and very probably encroached on their big house.

In 1910 Ed King was building a two-story, poured rein-forced-concrete house on the New River on the lot next to his cottage. This was a substantial house, probably at least the equiv-alent of King's original large home and an appropriate replace-ment as a family residence. The following anecdotal informa-tion from King's son-in-law, Bloxom Cromartie, gives useful evi-dence but also blurs the reality. Referring to King's rock pit lease, Cromartie recalled that "there was a quantity of small rock in the pit unwanted by the lessees. Deciding to pioneer concrete here, Cromartie mixed this with cement, using heavy reinforcing rods, and built the home for his bride (Louise King)."[95] Twenty-eight-year-old Cromartie was an up-and-coming young businessman, but he was no builder, and the improvements were certainly engineered and undertaken by Ed King. There was likely some understanding that the Kings would share the residence with the newly-weds. Bloxom Cromartie and Louise King were married in October 1909, the first formal wedding in Fort Lauderdale, and the young couple lived in another house just west of the King property while they waited for the new house to be finished.[96] Ed King had put in an eighty-two-foot private well on the property with a water tower to provide running water (and bathrooms) as well as carbide lighting (amenities the same as Bryan's Hotel) to be shared by both of the adjoining King homes.[97] At some point Ed King also upgraded the cottage to make it a comfortable res-idence, attaching the kitchen to the house and a small bathroom on the first floor. This may have been prior to or concurrent with the major renovation in 1911 when he added the second story with two bedrooms and a bathroom, creating the residence that we see today as the King-Cromartie House.[92]

It is difficult to pin down the exact transition process of the family from their original setting to the New River site. As of April 1910 the whole family, with the exception of newly-mar-ried Louise, was apparently still functioning as a unit and not living at the New River location. This conclusion is drawn from a census puzzle. The King family, other than Louise, was absent from the 1910 Federal Census sheets submitted on April 19, 1910 for the Fort Lauderdale area. An exhaustive search of the on-line Federal Census records using every conceivable form of the names (Edwin, Ed, E.T.; Susan or her preferred Clifford; E. Bird or Bird; Wallace; Eleanore or Eleanor) failed to find them anywhere in the U.S. Louise King Cromartie and her husband Bloxom are listed, and we know they were renting a house near the King's New River site waiting for their construction to be completed. Other family members should have shown up on the same listing if they had been living at the New River site also.

In November 1910 Susan King platted a corner of the King property for the Evergreen Cemetery.[98] Susan took the legal action because the deeds for the original purchases were in Susan's name only, but it is assumed that the cemetery was of mutual interest to both the Kings. One source has noted that "King often crafted caskets in his New River boat-building shop. He then transported the caskets—and sometimes the bodies—in his mule-drawn, hearse-like wagon, prompting some residents to call him 'the undertaker'." [99] The Cemetery was a commercial venture. Single plots sold for about $8, and a family plot with six gravesites went for $50. In June 1917 shortly after Fort Lauderdale transitioned from a town to a city with a new charter, the city purchased this seven-acre cemetery. The original platting shows that this is the segment of the 1904 purchase that was west of the rock pit. The comparable segment of the 1895 purchase adjoining to the south was undoubtedly the site of the King's large house. That land was eventually purchased by the city and incorporated into the Evergreen cemetery we see today.

The scope of the rock pit in 1910 is uncertain. The King's had leased it to the Hutton-Gladden Co. as of 1910.[95] An internet search on the company name found this 1911 statement: "The Hutton-Gladden Company of Fort Lauderdale, Fla, has purchased the stone quarries and equipment of R E McDonald at Fulford Fla., and will consolidate the business with the Fort Lauderdale quarries."[100] This suggests that the King rock pit was an up-and coming operation, more than would be comfortable in one's backyard. So, with good portions of their original Fort Lauderdale property converting to a cemetery and quarry, and the remainder mostly mangrove swamp extending into New River Sound, there seems to have been good reason for the King family to be moving on by the end of 1910. That would be consistent with Susan King's recollection of having lived in her big house for twelve years. A pamphlet prepared by the Junior League in cooperation with the City of Fort Lauderdale (1974) stated that Ed King's house "located south of Tarpon Bend was sold and later destroyed by fire."[92]

This transitional milestone in 1910 is a good point to reflect on what had been happening in the Ed King family. Ed and Susan Clifford King had been married for almost ten years when they settled as a family in Ft. Lauderdale in 1896. Though Susan was seven years junior, she was likely the captain of the union, and they probably made a pretty good team in the earlier years. It may well have been Susan's ambition that eased Ed out of a farming mode into the Flagler contacts and more lucrative building opportunities. Susan may have handled savings accounts or may have had funds from her family, but a first clue that we have of her position in the partnership is that the deeds for the initial purchases of land in Fort Lauderdale were in Susan's name only. This is a little surprising, though not highly unusual, and it may be less a reflection of Susan's dominance than a reflection of Ed's lack of concern or interest in property ownership. The first few years in Fort Lauderdale were probably very satisfying as the Kings, including brother Dick, focused on the homesite, developing the agricultural base and building the grand home that became the social hub for the whole area. Susan probably had pretty good control, and she may have encouraged Ed to take on the Adams building project and pursue boat-building. However, after brother Dick King left around 1900, the pressures certainly mounted on Ed King to take more management responsibility for the farm as he was continuing to get more and more involved in major building of boats and houses. Ed probably did not follow through sufficiently on the homefront, and probably did not manage his businesses efficiently. This led to confrontation and conflict at home, which he hated, encouraging him to stay away more as he had good reason with his building and dredging. Susan's resentments would have built as she struggled to deal with the farm property, and she would have felt increasingly isolated as the downtown hub developed over a mile away. How their farm eventually became a rock pit is a big question, but it is easy to imagine some trauma and drama as the relevant decisions played out. These are the kinds of tensions that can evolve in any marriage, but knowing that Ed and Susan eventually led separate lives, it is easy to presume that the marriage became progressively rockier as they moved through Ed's peak building period. Also, these tensions would have been very much at play as they transitioned from the original large house to the New River frontage properties, and it may explain the lack of clarity about the motivations, the sequencing and the conflicting reports about who lived where and when. It may not have been totally clear to them either as the situation evolved.

In 1910 Ed King was forty-seven, Susan (or Clifford, as she preferred) was forty, the "baby" Eleanore was sixteen, Wallace eighteen, Louise (newly married) twenty-one. Bird was married by October and turned twenty-three at the end of the year. Bird later recalled happy years in the early days in Fort Lauderdale with evenings of story-telling and games.[81] It is easy to imagine Ed's spontaneous personality creating such an environment. Ed's free spirit was the antithesis of control, so he was undoubtedly easy and supportive with his children, not much of a disciplinarian, and he encouraged self-sufficiency. Bird would have benefitted from early continuity with his dad as they built boats and got established on the water. As Ed's outside activities became more consuming, the burden for running the family obviously shifted to Susan, and while that may have resulted in resentments on her part, the children probably viewed this more with regret that they did not see their father often enough. In an era when strict family behavior was the norm, the King children had to

recognize that their father was an exception. He provided accep-
tance, though maybe not closeness, and his consistent leadership
in establishing and growing the local school system was constant
evidence that he was always working for their best interests. By
1910 the family was pretty well launched, though staying close
to home. Eleanore had probably finished high school. Bird was
definitely working at the family boat yard and Wallace probably
was also. In fact, the name of the yard was King Sons Co., Marine
Ways & Boat Works. Louise had attended the State Normal School
at Gainesville and had become a teacher in Ft. Lauderdale at age
seventeen,[101] so she had taught maybe three years before marry-
ing Bloxom Cromartie in October 1909. Information otherwise
about the young family members is extremely sketchy over the
next decade. Wallace joined the Coast Guard during World War
I and patrolled the beach by motorcycle;[102] Eleanore became a
nurse, but not until 1919.[103] It is easy to assume that during all
the unaccounted-for time the New River property provided a
convenient base as needed, and in effect it was a launching pad
for the family members.

Against this backdrop of evolving family, Ed King maintained
his involvement with the local schools. The Dade County School
Board instituted a new system for local school supervision as of
January 1907 by appointing a local citizen to be the supervisor. Ed
King was appointed to a two-year term for the Fort Lauderdale
white school. He next emerges in April 1910 appearing before the
School Board with Tom Bryan to plead for a new school because
of the influx of new students. The Board allotted $5,000 toward
the construction of a $7,000 two-story concrete structure, school
patrons making up the difference. The structure to be ready in
the fall of 1911 would have the beginnings of a high school with
the addition of a ninth grade. The new school would be built on
the site of the old two-room structure and would necessitate moving the old school.[104] All of this was "old hat" for Ed King by then.

Ed King built at least one more substantial structure during
this time period, another concrete-reinforced residence on
the Weidling property adjoining his near the river.[67] He also

undertook smaller jobs. Stout has noted that "well before (1913) Ed, Dick and Ralph King had installed baths and toilets in several local homes. They were builders, not plumbers, but in the absence of plumbers they plumbed."[105] And on "December 6, 1911: Contractor E. T. King is making rapid progress on the pedestrian passageway on the county bridge. Several accidents there stirred the county commission to action."[106]

All of this King family scenario was playing against a lively community background. The tempo of general activity in Fort Lauderdale was on a sharp upward trajectory, fueled by the Everglade dredging and its promise of expanded farmlands. The already robust agricultural production, and the wealth it was generating, supported a speculation fever geared to the prospect for cheap new land. This provided great stimulus to the local leaders to prepare for the advantages and get organized for the problems. Ed King was an obvious participant in the community process. In December 1910 E. T. King and W. H. Marshall were named to a committee to host a visit of the new Governor. In March 1911, the townsmen voted to incorporate the town and elected officers: W. H. Marshall, mayor; E. T. King, Council President; and Tom Bryan and three others, Councilmen. In 1913 Ed King and Tom Bryan were both members of a committee to push for the formation of a new county. The group was successful at the state level, but the issue was defeated in local referendums. Also in 1913, Ed King and Tom Bryan were among the fifteen incorporators of a Deep Water Harbor Company that worked with the U.S. Corps of Engineers on plans for a deep harbor with appropriate ocean access. This likewise met resistance that killed the idea. Then in 1913 elections for town government Ed King was not re-elected to the Council, very possibly by his own choice. Tom Bryan remained on the council and played a key role in 1915 in brokering state legislation leading to the formation of Broward County with Fort Lauderdale as the county seat.[107]

The establishment of the new county coincided with the completion of yet another bigger school for the burgeoning school population in Fort Lauderdale, so the two-story concrete school that Ed King had built less than 5 years before was available for new occupants. Ed King is credited with making the renovations and adjustments to turn this building into the first Broward County Courthouse.[67]

Prior to the school/courthouse makeover Ed King had completed the final building on the Bryan riverfront campus with the construction of the P.N. Bryan home north of the New River Hotel in 1914.[56] After these two projects, Ed King faded from view as an active public participant in Fort Lauderdale. His boatworks continued for at least another decade, for Bird continued to work there through the Boom.[81] Ed King may have undertaken some lesser building, but his attention and presence were being drawn to Torrey Island in the evolving community of Belle Glade at the edge of Lake Okeechobee.

In trying to understand how the rest of Ed King's life played out, it helps to consider who Ed King, the man, was in 1915. Building things must have come as naturally to Ed King as getting out of bed. Add a good work ethic, and it is easy to see how he could focus and get consumed in any project, whether houses, boats, or dredges. He had an uncanny ability to make things, take them apart or move them. He must have had a generous amount of the innate capacity to internally visualize a three-dimensional form and its component parts. His ability to see things in total context made it easy for Ed King to extend beyond woodworking to masonry materials or water and lighting systems or dredging strategies. None would dispute that Ed King was one very capable guy.

The essence of Ed King, though, is not in his capabilities, but how they were applied. Given a different personality he might have been a Flagler, but Ed was fundamentally a free spirit and a most selfless man. He did not like to be boxed in. He was stimulated by the challenge of new frontiers, whether geographic or technological, and he was drawn to people of power and wealth because they could make things happen. He enjoyed serving them, but there is no evidence that he was personally driven to seek power or wealth. In fact, the evidence is to the contrary.

Tom Bryan recalled in 1962 that Ed King was "the most accommodating man ever, (who) made himself available whenever he was needed. He was capable of any project. There was no one to match his ability as a carpenter. King built houses. This was his main occupation, but he was called on for many odd jobs—such as outer cases for coffins, and when a family couldn't afford the price of a coffin, he'd contribute his time and material and build the coffin."[45] The overall picture of Ed King was that of an optimistic, happy man who was eager to make other people happy. He was a friend to everyone.

The other side of this coin is that Ed King undoubtedly avoided confrontation, disliked conflict, was a hands-off manager, a poor businessman, and a worse politician. He did not like to run things, and the success he had in his various ventures most probably resulted from the fact that he was a good teacher, and he relied on good training for his staff so they could take on the responsibilities themselves. A more obscure part of Ed King's legacy as a builder in Fort Lauderdale is not only that he was the first and best, but he also trained the next echelon of builders. Both Frank Oliver and Tom Bryan worked with Ed early in their careers and then became major builders and developers of downtown Fort Lauderdale. In any case, Ed King's qualities may have played well with the outside world, but they created problems at home beginning long before 1915. As responsibilities mounted, Ed's discomforts with control put a lot of pressure on Susan. She apparently coped very well, and may have enjoyed the responsibilities, but she lost patience with a loose-cannon husband, and they both functioned best if they stayed away from each other.

Ed King's separation from his family probably just happened—not a big decision or strategy and maybe not intended to be permanent. He was just ready to move on. The children were all doing their own thing, and Susan was not about to leave all she had worked for in Fort Lauderdale. They likely reached an amiable truce with Susan taking control, if she did not already have it, of their resources in Fort Lauderdale. Several factors likely propelled Ed's decision to leave. As Fort Lauderdale matured into a city Ed must have felt stifled by the administrative trivia, the contentious issues, the politics, and the swarms of new people coming in and taking over to push their own agendas. In contrast, Ed had espoused the dream for years of fertile land to be had at the edge of the Everglades and was obviously convinced that there was real opportunity there. Another factor had to be his changing eyesight. He was nearly blind by the time he died,[76] and that condition was likely a gradual deterioration. He may well have tapered off his building activities because he could simply not see well enough to maintain his standards. He certainly would have dreaded any dependency situation, and farming was a much more feasible activity for maintaining his independence. But the factor that may have brought this together was the involvement with his siblings and parents. Ed's father and mother and youngest brother Dwight established themselves as truck farmers in nearby Dania,[82] and brother Dick was in the general area for some years. Sister Margaret may already have been at Torrey Island near Belle Glade on the fringes of Lake Okeechobee in Palm Beach County. That was Ed's point of refuge. A contributing event that would have brought the whole family together was the death of Ed King's father in June 1917. It was not long after that that Ed King was growing onions on Torrey Island.[108]

Young family members were getting settled. Bird's 1917 military draft registration shows that he was a self-employed boat builder in Fort Lauderdale with a wife and child. Wallace finished his U.S. military service, attaining the rank of Sgt., and by 1919 had a cycle shop on Brickell Avenue. Eleanor in 1919 graduated as a trained nurse from the Atlanta College of Medicine in Georgia. In the 1920 census, (Susan) Clifford King, Wallace and Eleanore are listed as residents in the household of Bloxom and Louise Cromartie on South River Street in Ft. Lauderdale, presumably in the large house. Ed King is found in the Ritta precinct of Palm Beach County that included Belle Glades and Torrey Island. Ed was property owner and head of household, the other members being Ed's sister Margaret, her husband and three daughters. Ed categorized himself as truck farmer, and he had probably been there at least three years by that time. In April 1918 correspondence to Frank Stranahan from Torrey Island Ed tells of harvesting nine and a half acres of onions.[108] The time factors involved in tilling and planting the crop would place the planting in 1917.

This arrangement of separate living continued for more than ten years, years of dramatic Boom and Bust in all of South Florida driven by a frenzy of land speculation. Early in the 1920s both Wallace and Eleanore were married, so the King family residents on the New River site dropped down to three: Louise and Bloxham Cromartie and Susan King. Subsequent actions suggest that the family in 1925 was feeling an economic pinch or taking defensive actions in anticipation of the downturn. That year Bird moved to Miami because of the Bust, suggesting that the Boat Works either closed or was sold.[81] Also that year the Cromarties or Kings sold the concrete house on the River,[95] and Susan and the Cromarties all took up residence in the King-Cromartie House. The following year was the year of the devastating 1926 Hurricane that wiped out neighboring Hollywood and caused serious damage in Fort Lauderdale. A number of reports indicate that Ed King's various structures were resilient to the natural forces, and there is no record of any problems for the King family, but the already limping economy took another hit. Two years later in September 1928 another hurricane hit farther north around Palm Beach, sparing Fort Lauderdale major damage, but as it moved inland over Lake Okeechobee it became one of the most deadly tropical storms in US history. The storm surge forced a cascade of water over the southern edge of the lake, sweeping away numerous houses and buildings. At least 2,500 people drowned. Ed King was among them. Only Ed's sister Margaret survived from that household.[72] As tragic as this ending is, it may have been a fitting exit for a free-spirited Ed King who was gradually sinking into the bondage of blindness and inevitable dependency. Ed King had just turned sixty-five at the time of his death. He was remembered fondly by many and given much credit and recognition for his trailblazing accomplishments in creating and building Fort Lauderdale.

Ed King's death probably did not change much of anything for the family. Certainly they felt the loss, and they may have gained some new appreciation of what their husband/father represented, but they were already used to the separation. Bird had already settled into boat-building in Miami,[81] and Wallace had established himself as a yacht captain. Eleanore had married and started a family while pursuing a nursing career. Susan and the Cromarties continued to live in the upgraded cottage on the New River. Within another year the stock market crashed and an already reeling Fort Lauderdale sank into the Depression that hit the whole country. The concrete house on the New River returned to the family in 1929 through a foreclosure, and the family took control of it again until it was eventually sold to the Hydes and became know as the Hyde House.[95] The Cromarties apparently stayed in the smaller house and Susan in the larger structure. In the 1930 census Susan King is listed right next to Bloxom Cromartie, both Heads of Household and property owners, Susan's property valued at $8,000 and Cromartie's valued at $2,500. Susan moved back in with the Cromarties when the larger house sold, and stayed there until her death in 1939. The Cromarties continued to live there. Bloxom died in 1952, and Louise remained in the house for some years. A September 1968 clipping reported that "Byrd King, Mrs. Louise King Cromartie's brother, who moved to Miami in 1925, has returned, his wife having died, and is living with his sister in the old home on S River Dr."[109] That did not last very long for the house was sold soon after to a developer who intended to clear the property.[110] A community effort to save the house for its historical significance resulted in a successful campaign to move the house upriver to the Historical Society site by the New River Inn. This was accomplished in 1971.[111] Two of the King children participated in the various events associated with this re-location. Wallace had died prematurely in 1935, and Louise had withdrawn from public activity, but Bird and Eleanor were featured guests in the celebrations. Louise died not long afterward, in 1973; Eleanor lived until 1978; and Bird lived to the age of ninety-two in 1980.

The King-Cromartie house is the most personal reminder we have of the King family and its place in Fort Lauderdale history. Other monuments of Ed King's building attest to Ed's skill as a builder, but the little house embodies a story of family evolution. They built it together and they all lived there at one time or another as that house emerged from a convenience pad to house of refuge. In the 1907–1911 timeframe during which the house took the full form that we see today, Bird was nineteen to twenty-three and Wallace was fifteen to nineteen. Though they were otherwise occupied, as was their father, they must have participated in the building process. The young family members were undoubtedly also early users. It was a nice walk to the boatworks. It was also an easy walk to the school, so at a minimum the house was a convenient stop-off point for the girls as student and teacher. Early on this house was probably Ed King's preferred pad, while Susan likely preferred the big house, but the little house became the fall-back position even up to the end when Bird returned from Miami. That was more than a sixty year span filled with one family's experience, full of the joys and sorrows that make up lifetimes. It was a respectable, unpretentious and very practical little house that is probably more representative of the evolving town and city of Fort Lauderdale than Ed King's other landmarks that represent exceptions for their time. It is also probably the best representation of who Edwin T. King really was. For all his free spirit, trailblazing and joy of living, Ed King was a very respectable, unpretentious and practical man—with a very big heart.

5

Other Key Players

The Marshall Families and Other Growers

The first real infusion of settlers into the Fort Lauderdale template consisted almost entirely of growers. We have already seen that fruit and vegetable production was the initial objective for the Kings and the Bryans. Beginning in 1895 there was a steady flow of newcomers, less like a wave than a consistently rising tide that quietly spreads out. They were here to recoup their losses from a natural weather catastrophe. They were experienced and hardworking, and they knew their business, whether growing fruit or vegetables. Their energy went into their labors, and they kept a low profile as far as the community was concerned. They quickly learned that tomatoes were the profitable crop. It did not require much investment in land or equipment, and it was highly rewarding. Success was almost immediate, and the wealth that was created fueled a whole new economy.

The earliest grower was Lewis W. Marshall who was followed by several family members, so the Marshall name became very prominent. Lewis came in 1895 with an older brother, Uncle Billy, as an employee of Thomas H. White, founder and president of the White Sewing Machine Company of Cleveland. Lewis was paid $25 per month.[112] Here is an account: "The Marshalls were brought here by Thomas H. White, the sewing machine man, to farm his lands here. The first crop, tomatoes and squash, was shipped to New York and Philadelphia and brought high prices. There were no produce buyers here that early, all truck (produce) shipped on consignment."[113] Another source has claimed that when the first train reached Ft. Lauderdale in February 1896, White/Marshall had a consignment of tomatoes on the platform ready for shipment north.[114] This could only have been accomplished at that time by someone with the know-how and connections of the White Co. How long the White/Marshall relationship continued is uncertain. Subsequent sources give no mention of the White Co. as a grower, and Lewis Marshall purchased his property from Thomas White, 360 acres according to a family source.[112] That may have been White's total holding, and after one prosperous season, White may have withdrawn. Following is a possible scenario.

Lewis Marshall was a fruit grower in central Florida when the great freeze wiped out the grove he had established in 1890. He was thirty-two years old with a family of four children, two older boys, ten and seven, and two younger daughters. Lewis had a history of moving around. He was a Georgia boy who had sought excitement in Texas, married there, and stayed awhile before returning to Georgia and on to central Florida. With the disaster of the freeze, Lewis was ready to pack up and go again. It is unclear how he made the contact with White, but it is clear that when he went to Fort Lauderdale he was intending to stay. He and his brother Bill, fifteen years older, made the trip on a mule-drawn wagon containing the family possessions. The family came later by train to West Palm Beach and boat on to Fort Lauderdale.[115]

The property Lewis eventually settled on, which presumably was White's property, was on the only segment of the New River's South Fork that Mary Brickell did not own. This was Section Sixteen by geological survey description, and this section, plus the one immediately to the south, had been part of a failed marketing scheme of 1887 to create a platted Palm City. National marketing of lots and tracts had not been successful enough to carry through with development. Though property had been sold, the concept folded.[116] It seems possible that Thomas White was an investor in that project and was seeking a way to add value to it to recoup his investment. There is no indication he was interested in farming, but he had to make the land produce, hence the arrangement with Lewis Marshall.

Big acreage is not the customary way to start growing tomatoes and other vegetables, and there was virtually no local labor supply, so Lewis Marshall quickly established himself as a sharecropping agent. He brought in members of his family and imported other help during the growing season. He would bring families from Georgia every year to help on the farm as share croppers, furnishing them a house to live in.[112] This is reflected in a November 1898 newspaper account: "L. W. Marshall has 75 acres of fine rich land, mostly hammock (high ground) on the south fork, about 25 acres of which has been cleared. Mr. Marshall is fast making a model place. He will make a crop of 10 acres of tomatoes and one acre of mixed vegetables. The following crop will also be made by different parties upon his land: George Brabham, 2 acres tomatoes and 1 acre peppers and beans; J. S. Boyd, 2 acres tomatoes; Thomas Powell, 3 acres tomatoes; J. E. Marshall, 3 acres of tomatoes; J. W. Marshall and J. R. Marsh, 2 acres eggplants; Wm. Marshall, 1 ½ acres tomatoes."[20]

An early landmark on the South Fork of the New River was Marshall's packinghouse. It was a large, barn-like structure rising to three levels at the peak. It was built partially over the water to facilitate loading and unloading for river transport, and very likely for ready disposal of waste. There is no doubt that Lewis Marshall enjoyed great and continuing success. He would take his family to Georgia for the summer, the off-season, and they had a home there. Otherwise, he seemed to keep his focus on his agricultural pursuits. Unfortunately, his tenure in Ft. Lauderdale was cut short after only a dozen years by his untimely death at age forty-three of kidney disease. At that point his boys were eighteen and twenty-one, and neither of them carried on in their father's stead. However, the Marshall name did not fade from the local growers' scene. Lewis had two nephews who had come into the area in 1899 who were playing dominant roles. Nephew Mack Marshall was active in Dania, just south of Fort Lauderdale, and Mack's brother William H. Marshall was well-established in Fort Lauderdale and on his way to becoming a key player in the town's development.[117]

William Marshall came to Ft. Lauderdale by way of Cuba. As a patriotic, red-blooded twenty-two-year-old he had responded to the call for volunteers for the Spanish-American War in 1898 and actually saw action in Cuba. Returning to Georgia to muster out in 1899 he stopped in Fort Lauderdale to check in on Uncle Lewis and Uncle Bill and brother Mack, and he was back in a hurry to participate in the opportunity here.[118] W.H. (William) Marshall got his start on Uncle Lewis's property, and as he prospered he began to accumulate acreage of his own. He was apparently buying land all over the place. A 1906 map shows him with fifty acres on the South Fork beyond his Uncle Lewis's seventy-five acres.[34] In 1913, when plans were underway for a deepwater port where the current yacht harbor is, "W. H. Marshall owned the property on the landward side of the proposed port and farmed there."[119] He eventually became one of the largest producers of commercial truck crops in this section of Florida. When supply began to catch up with demand, depressing prices, W. H. Marshall took a significant initiative to develop direct channels to northern markets, cutting out the regional brokers. "Through correspondence he opened northern outlets for surplus vegetables. Before long, his Marshall Produce Co. was shipping 98 percent of his crop to northern cities."[118]

William H. Marshall was a mover and shaper. He stands out among the growers who as a group kept a very low profile. He was an imposing figure, 6' 3", and he liked to be in charge. He obviously thought big, and he was committed to developing the town and local agricultural scene. He championed pertinent issues, like drainage and sea walls, and he enjoyed getting into the fray. He was probably more politically oriented than his peers, but he was more a driver than a charismatic leader. He was the new town's first mayor, though he was not re-elected after the first term. He was also the first State Representative from Broward County, serving two terms. He was a strong voice in the Board of Trade and served in various other public capacities during his active career. William Marshall was a champion of growers, and while others moved from being growers to broader interests, his priority shifted only from the local scene to the national. He spent much of 1927-1930 in Washington, D.C. lobbying for tariff protection for Florida growers.

Quick money from tomatoes became a big draw for early Fort Lauderdale. For many it was the springboard to other pursuits. Here is some anecdotal information to illustrate. A young Carl Mattox arrived in 1900, bought 130 acres, cleared five and started growing tomatoes. He had the property about paid for after two seasons, so he sold 125 acres, including the five he had cultivated, to Frank Oliver and W. O. Berryhill. High water in 1902 did not affect the five acres now cultivated by Oliver and Berryhill, and they got a high price for the crop. Within the year they sold to H. G. Wheeler and cleared about $3,000 each. This motivated Mattox, who still had five acres, to put that in production. He invited Ed Peele, a friend from Atlanta, to come down and help work that land for $18 a month and board. In the off-season, both Mattox and Peele got jobs running one of Ed King's dredges on the intracoastal waterway. Mattox decided to stay with dredging, and Peele went back to share-crop Mattox's land. Peele began to use his off-season time hunting alligators in the Everglades. He would clear $2,500 to $4,000 on his tomatoes and pick up $500 to $600 more from gator hides. Eventually he bought his own land, and later became groundskeeper for the Golf and Country Club.[120]

There were very few in early Fort Lauderdale whose lives were not affected one way or another by tomato growing. Quite apart from providing the general wealth, this activity provided leverage and stimulus for almost everything else. Growers may not have contributed high drama, but they created momentum, and they made Fort Lauderdale start moving.

Stranahan and Oliver and Other Businessmen

The business community was very slow to develop in early Fort Lauderdale. Frank Stranahan's one-stop service center with camp and store pre-dated the need, and Frank was very good at keeping up with demand, so for several years there was little pressure or incentive for alternatives. Frank provided good service, whatever the needs were; he was liked; he was trusted; and he kept every-one's accounts. It meant, of course, that Stranahan's operation be-came very large, and it was close to a decade before the economic hub of Fort Lauderdale moved from Frank's county road site to the railroad site a half-mile upstream. Frank's own expansion created the first noticeable changes, first at the ferry-crossing site and then at the railroad dock. Gradually other providers began getting established at the railroad hub, and a main street began forming on Brickell Avenue. By 1911, substantial structures lined Brickell Avenue and extended one block east to Andrews Avenue. The area around the rail hub had been transformed in about five years. Merchants and hoteliers had taken the lead.

Stranahan, of course, led the way. Frank had been hired as the paid attendant of a camp owned by his cousin Guy Metcalf, but before he arrived on the job the idea of adding a store was already a serious consideration. While still in Melbourne, where he had been working for several years, Frank was in discussion with a Boston-based investor interested in building and stocking a small store. All the initiative appears to have been from the investor. Stranahan arrived at the New River site at the end of January 1893. In May 1893 lumber and store inventory were shipped on a schooner from Jacksonville, but the vessel wrecked. The cargo was lost, and the investor withdrew. The ensuing six months was a period of considerable uncertainty because of financial issues for Guy Metcalf as well as the Brickell issues of diverting the county road and moving the overnight camp. All of this was ap-parently sorted out by the summer of 1894, though the details are not clear. However, by then Frank had become a property owner, achieved his independence of Guy Metcalf, and was licensed by the county to operate the ferry. The idea of a store was then pursued with the Lyman family of Palm Beach. The Lymans may well have raised the subject. They were already operating a trading-post store in Lantana, the northern terminus of the county road. Lyman family sources have stated that two Lyman brothers owned at least fifty percent of Stranahan and Co. in early years, though little else is known about the relationship. Most certainly Frank received good tutelage on inventories, store procedures, supply channels and banking connections. A permanent trading post building went up, probably in 1895 after Ed King arrived. This structure was added to almost constantly as business grew and grew. On the other hand the overnight camp lost its regular customers once the railroad was operational in 1896. The stage line did not last very long after that, though the camp continued to serve a useful purpose as the only temporary lodging available in the area. Also, the ferry offered the only vehicular crossing of the New River, and that quickly became an essential service as the area began to grow. So, the ferry franchise kept Frank Stranahan tethered to the county road site, and the ferry crossing became the focus of Frank's first expansion.[83]

The years 1900 and 1901 were game-changing years for Frank Stranahan. He appeared to be acting on his own without ties to the Lyman brothers; he brought in his brother Will to help run the store and keep the books; he married the town's first schoolteacher, Ivy Cromartie; he hired W. O. Berryhill and B. A. (Bloxom) Cromartie, Ivy's brother, as permanent staff in the store; and he undertook a major construction project, building a small cottage for himself and Ivy and replacing the trading post with a two-story building (now known as Stranahan House).

This looks like progress and may suggest a degree of sophistication creeping in, but here is an anecdote to remind how rustic early Fort Lauderdale was: Berryhill and Cromartie, young twenty-year-olds, slept in the unfinished upper level of the new store. "The Seminoles always were welcome to sleep on the Stranahan porch. When the mosquitoes were bad, Berryhill and Cromartie would wake to find their bedroom floor covered with sleeping Indians, driven inside. Fleas, blamed on Indian dogs, were a plague second to none." "Every two weeks, the bachelors Berryhill and Cromartie would clear their bedroom for a dance, the music supplied by a fiddle and a guitar."[94]

More changes were brewing in 1902. Frank's brother Will, described as "of a rambling nature," was probably gone before the end of 1902, increasing the involvement and responsibilities of Berryhill and Cromartie. By 1903 trade at the store had so increased the business was incorporated. Shareholders in addition to Frank Stranahan were W.O. Berryhill, B.A. Cromartie and Frank Oliver.[83] Frank Oliver's involvement probably represents venture capital. Oliver was a shrewd businessman, not a mercantilist. He came into the area early (1895), seemingly involved in most any activity where there was a quick profit. Among other things he became a principal grower, and a major builder and developer. The incorporation of Stranahan and Company might well have been driven by Frank, and it seems very possible that his participation was with the understanding that he would proceed to build a store at the railroad dock. That is what happened in 1903. In December 1903 the *Miami Metropolis* reported that the Stranahan Co. "has just completed a store near the depot, 32 x 75 feet, with a capacious hall above. He is the postmaster and will move the office very soon to his new building, where it will be much more convenient to the patrons."[28] The deed for Stranahan's purchase of the building site is dated January 1904, but we have plenty of examples of deeds dated well-after relevant action on the ground.

There was little more than a boxcar train station at the railway dock on the east side of the tracks when Stranahan's store was going up. However, facing the river on the west side of the tracks was the Bryan Hotel, already a flourishing establishment, described in the Bryan narrative. By the time Stranahan's store was occupied in 1904, the Bryan's were engaged in their major construction project of moving the frame hotel and building two masonry residences as well as a large, three-story masonry hotel.

The year 1904 also saw the construction of the first vehicular bridge across the New River at Andrews Ave., two blocks east of the railroad bridge. Stranahan's new store on the north bank of the New River would become the anchor for a downtown Fort Lauderdale extending north up Brickell Avenue and east to Andrews Avenue.

The second large building on Brickell Avenue, probably under construction in 1904, was erected by the Osceola Fruit and Vegetable Company. This structure, a block north of Stranahan's, was intended to be "the largest and best equipped packinghouse on the East Coast."[28] The building is prominent in all early pictures of the railway docks, but there is no indication of how much it was used, and it would eventually become the Osceola Hotel.

All early pictures of the railway dock show a small "Restaurant" building on the river's edge at the end of the dock, the back part of the building supported by pilings in the river. Mary Brickell in 1905 leased the riparian rights for this location to A.B. Waites who established a bakery/restaurant. The Waites' lived in a boxcar across the dock from the restaurant, also apparent in the early photos. This boxcar had served as the first railway station, and when the permanent station was built, the Waites bought the boxcar and remodeled it for a residence.[121]

In 1907 W.C. Kyle arrived in Fort Lauderdale as the newly assigned FEC station agent. He was soon involved in local commerce as the owner and proprietor of the Everglades Grocery store, an early structure on Brickell Avenue between Stranahan's and the Osceola building.[122] The grocery was probably built about the time of a major expansion of Stranahan's. An August 1908 press report stated that "Stranahan & Co. is preparing to build a store addition on the rear of the already large store."[84] Early pictures show this to be a two-story wing at the rear, making an L-shaped building. The lap of the "L" was then filled in with a one-story slant-roof component.

Earlier in 1908 the Bryan's new hotel, the New River Hotel, opened for business just after the first of the year. This was Fort Lauderdale's most upscale facility, boasting two bathrooms and carbide lighting, a large lounge and large dining room, and twenty-five spacious guest rooms. About the same time Frank Oliver built a smaller, less pretentious masonry hotel, the Keystone Hotel, on Andrews Avenue at the first cross-street up from the river, Wall Street. Within another year the transformation of the Osceola packinghouse into the Osceola Hotel was in progress, and by 1911 that hotel was a major presence on Brickell Avenue where Wall Street intersected.

A change in Stranahan & Co. leadership in 1910 was the trigger for another new store. Berryhill and Cromartie sold their interests, very likely to Frank Oliver, formed their own general merchandising business, and put up a two-story masonry building on Andrews Avenue where the bridge crossed the river. There is no hint that this competitive move was viewed negatively within the company. It may well have been encouraged, part of a scenario played out in 1911. Frank Oliver bought out Frank Stranahan. The succeeding company was The Oliver Bros. Co.[83] Frank Oliver's younger brother, David, a recent Phi Beta Kappa graduate of the University of North Carolina, had joined Frank and another brother in Ft. Lauderdale in 1910. David Oliver was eventually General Manager of the Oliver Bros. store.[123]

A significant step up for the emerging community in 1910 was the chartering of the town's first bank. Stranahan & Co. had been the town's financial center from the beginning. Frank's ledgers of credits and debits kept track of a large cashless credit system, and Frank's bank, the First National Bank of St. Augustine, was the main channel for cash flow. Frank turned to his bank for advice when proposals for a bank first surfaced. He was cautioned not to resist it, but either take control of it himself or stay out of it in a benign way.[83] It is not surprising that Frank chose the latter course. Frank was not highly competitive nor confrontational. On the other hand, Frank Oliver, his partner at the time, never missed a good opportunity. Frank Oliver put up half the funds required to obtain a charter; Tom Bryan, who was the organizer, put up the other half; and Frank Oliver was named Bank President on his condition that he did not have to be involved in running the bank.[40] Once the bank was functional, Frank Stranahan was relieved of a big community responsibility, and his accounts reverted to normal business accounting. Whether it was part of a plan or just circumstances, this change may have been a factor in Stranahan's selling out to Oliver in 1911. In so doing, Frank Stranahan removed himself from his traditional role in the community.

In 1911 the competition for retail in Ft. Lauderdale was tightened significantly with the entry of H. G. Wheeler on the scene. He was an experienced official with the Flagler organization, and he and his wife had been periodic sojourners in Fort Lauderdale. After leaving Flagler's service, he moved here permanently to establish a store that would give Frank Stranahan a run for his money. Wheeler put up a store facing the New River right across the street (Brickell Avenue) from Stranahan & Co. It was a three-story concrete building that dwarfed most everything else around. People called it "Wheeler's Folly," and it opened for business around the end of 1911.[124]

The landscape was drastically altered in June 1912 when a fire wiped out the lower end of Brickell Avenue. The fire apparently started within Wheeler's store, so that fireproof cement structure was left as a stark skeleton. Stranahan's was completely leveled along with everything else up to Wall Street. Amazingly the Osceola Hotel, a tinderbox if there ever was one, survived, only to burn in singular glory just a year later.

Rapid rebuilding was testimony to the good economic health of the new town, and by 1913 the town was fully functioning again. Rebuilding coincided with the advent of electric service from Tom Bryan's power plant, so what resulted was a much more modern and mature-looking downtown. Brickell Avenue was nicely lined with attractive two and three-story masonry buildings with a substantial Oliver Brothers store anchoring where Stranahan's had been, and the Stranahan name was gone from the scene. Wheeler participated in the rebuilding, but never again with the flair exhibited on his entry. New names appeared, and most old names found themselves in much nicer new work environments. It was a solid base for the significant growth that would continue for more than another decade.

6

The Legacy and Shifting Scene

The preceding family stories extend beyond "early Fort Lauderdale." That period, for the purposes of this narrative, is the twenty years from 1897 to 1917. In 1897 Fort Lauderdale was little more than a trading post, postal drop, a boxcar train station and a town plat. In 1917 Fort Lauderdale was newly chartered by the state as a city, upgraded from a town with extended boundaries. The intervening time period was characterized by a sharp focus on Fort Lauderdale as an agricultural center; the beach was essentially irrelevant. In 1917 Fort Lauderdale created its first roadway to the beach, conquering the mangrove swamp barrier. That opened up new horizons and stimulated new visions of what Fort Lauderdale could become, and it would never be the same again.

Our narrative has featured the earliest settlers who provided the leadership that shaped the emerging community. With one exception they were men who were eager to take action and make things happen, not afraid to take the lead and face the risks. Bryan, King, Marshall and Oliver were instigators and initiators. In contrast Stranahan was a facilitator and responder, but, by virtue of his being in the area first, he provided critical services that were crucial to the smooth evolution of Fort Lauderdale. No one individual dominated. It was a cooperative effort that moved and shaped the emerging community. From the beginning everyone worked well together, and that did not change when political framework was finally established. The ablest men were elected to office and were ready to serve. That is the real legacy of the early settlers, because it is still that way. Politics in Fort Lauderdale has remained essentially non-partisan, and politicians here have a long tradition of working for the community good.

The population of Fort Lauderdale took a quantum leap between 1910 and 1920, from 143 to 2,065. New arrivals added significantly to the scope and diversity of businesses as well as to community leadership. Other movers and shapers became active as the city shifted to a broader vision as a tourist and retirement destination as well as an agricultural and business center. Early key players continued to take active roles in the ongoing scene into the late 1920s. On a personal level most of the early settlers had shifted away from their original pursuits and were focusing on real estate transactions. By 1925 they were nearly all millionaires, some many times over. The frenzy of land speculation throughout South Florida between 1920-1925 boosted the whole community to amazing heights, but the slide from Boom to Bust was already underway in 1926 and a major hurricane that fall spurred the decline. Over the next couple of years all the banks in town failed, wiping out most everyone's reserves and exposing tremendous indebtedness. Fort Lauderdale was in Depression a year before the national Depression. Frank Stranahan was a casualty, his despondency being a factor in his suicide. Most all the other old-timers withdrew from active participation in the local scene, and many of them had lost virtually everything. Tom Bryan and W.H. Marshall were notable exceptions.

Americans like to honor Heroes and Special Achievers. We in Fort Lauderdale have a problem identifying the significant players in our early history. Major Lauderdale was here barely long enough to leave his name. William and Mary Brickell technically founded the city, but they never lived here. Nevertheless, they bought it, defined the routing of major transportation arteries, and platted what is still city center. Frank Stranahan was first on the ground, but he was a service provider and not a definer. Things did not really take shape until the instigators and initiators came on the scene. There have been many over the years, but the names that stood out in the early years were the Bryans, Kings, Marshalls and Olivers. They were the first wave of movers and shapers, and of these Tom Bryan's record is the most extensive and comprehensive. Thomas Murray Bryan, without a doubt, was Fort Lauderdale's most influential pioneer.

Endnotes

1   August Burghard and Philip Weidling, *Checkered Sunshine*, rev.ed. (Fort Lauderdale: Wake-Brook House, 1974), 5-15."

2   Beth Brickell, *William and Mary Brickell: Founders of Miami and Fort Lauderdale*, (Charleston, SC: History Press, 2011), chap. 5.

3   Deed of Sale No. 391, dated August 1, 1890, microfilm numbers 089 and 090 from deed records provided by Dade County to Broward County for properties recorded in Dade County prior to 1915.

4   Wesley Stout, Beachcomber columns, *Fort Lauderdale News*: June 4, 1959; July 21, 1963; December 7, 1965; and September 17, 1968.

5   J. Kent Planck, "Big Boss: The Story of the Birches and the Roots, Part 3," *The Newsletter*, Bonnet House Museum and Gardens, January-March 2012, 1, 7.

6   Beth Brickell, Chapter 9.

7   J. L. "Sam" Heede, "Our Bryan Pioneers, Part II," *Broward Legacy* 8 (Winter/Spring 1985): 21-32

8   T. E. Fitzgerald, *Volusia County: Past and Present*, Observer Press, Daytona Beach, Florida, 1937.

9   F.W. DeCroix, *An Historical and Progressive Review of Miami. Fort Lauderdale and Other Sections in Dade County Florida*, Chapter LXIL, "Bryan's Hotel," 1911.

10 Beachcomber, September 18, 1960.

11 Beachcomber, April 5, 1959.

12 Beachcomber, December 10, 1959 and Wednesday April 17, 1959.

13 Beachcomber, Tuesday, November 5, 1957 and Friday, August 7, 1959.

14 Duane Jones, "Pioneer, Builder, Organizer Is Life Story of Tom Bryan," *Miami Herald*, March 14, 1954.

15 Beachcomber, October 1, 1961.

16 Stuart Bryan (grandson of P.N. Bryan), in conversation with the Fort Lauderdale Historical Society. The deed was delayed for some years because of tax issues.

17 Beachcomber, December 4, 1959.
18 "Old Bryan Grove," (Fort Lauderdale) *Free Press*, April 23, 1937.
19 Barbara A. Paleo, "Seminoles and Settlers: South Florida Perspectives 1890 – 1920", *Broward Legacy* 21 (Winter/Spring 1998): 22-25.
20 "Among the Farmers," *Broward Legacy* 9 (Summer/Fall 1986): 34, 35.
21 "Dade's Development," *Broward Legacy* 9 (Summer/Fall 1986): 36.
22 Douglas Kalajian, "His is Life and Times of Fort Lauderdale," *Miami Herald*, June 3, 1990.
23 Beachcomber, November 22, 1956.
24 Beachcomber, August 2, 1954.
25 Mrs. Camille Bryan, interview by Martha Brooks and Gene Avallone, March 31, 1976. Fort Lauderdale Historical Society.
26 William Bien, "Tom Bryan: Pioneer Business Leader," Trade Names, *Fort Lauderdale News*, undated clipping from 1958.
27 William Moore, <u>Tom Bryan, 90, Saw City Grow From Village of 250</u>, *Fort Lauderdale News and Sun-Sentinel*, October 6, 1968.
28 "Fort Lauderdale Growers," *Broward Legacy* 9 (Summer/Fall 1986): 41.
29 "From New River Hotel to Discovery Center," Fort Lauderdale Historical Society, unpublished information sheet, 1980.
30 Beachcomber, March 11, 1957.
31 Beachcomber, December 21, 1961.
32 Burghard and Weidling, 27.
33 Stuart McIver, "Dredging Up a Piece of History," The Way We Were, *Fort Lauderdale News and Sun-Sentinel*, Sunshine magazine, February 12, 1984.
34 "Excursion to Ft. Lauderdale: Harvest Home Picnic and Barbecue at Seminole Park, New River, May 22 06," handbill, Fort Lauderdale Historical Society Museum.
35 "Fort Lauderdale is Now Enjoying an Unprecedented Building Boom," *Miami Metropolis*, November 22, 1907.
36 Beachcomber, August 4, 1961.
37 Beachcomber, October 6, 1955.
38 Patrick Scott, "The Progresso Land Sale of 100 Years Ago," *Sun Sentinel*, March 19, 2011.
39 Burghard and Weidling, 29.
40 Beachcomber, February 25, 1955.
41 Burghard and Weidling, 33-36.
42 Burghard and Weidling, 38-41.
43 Beachcomber, July 3, 1962 and July 17, 1962.
44 Beachcomber, September 3, 1962 and February 14, 1954.
45 Tom Bryan, interview, Fort Lauderdale Historical Society, 1962.

46 Beachcomber, March 10, 1954
47 Beachcomber, April 1, 1955.
48 Susan Gillis, *Fort Lauderdale, the Venice of America*, Arcadia Publishing, Charleston, SC, 2004, 24.
49 Burghard and Weidling, 51.
50 Burghard and Weidling, 70.
51 Cooper Kirk, "The Failure to Create Broward County: 1913," *Broward Legacy* 11 (Summer/Fall 1988): 2-4.
52 Cooper Kirk, "The Struggle to Create Broward County: 1914-1915," *Broward Legacy* 11 (Summer/Fall 1988): 55.
53 Beachcomber, October 30, 1960.
54 Susan Gillis, 26.
55 Beachcomber, November 16, 1953 and November 27, 1956.
56 "Fort Lauderdale County Seat of Broward County," *Broward Legacy* 11 (Summer/Fall 1988): 18.
57 "(New River Inn) Facts and Interesting Notes," unpublished information sheet, Fort Lauderdale Historical Society.
58 *Fort Lauderdale Herald*, March 14, 1919.
59 Denyse Cunningham, "Broward County Sites on the National Register of Historical Places," Bryan Building, *Broward Legacy* 24 (Spring/Summer 2003): 17.
60 Beachcomber, June 3, 1954.
61 Burghard and Weidling, 118-121.
62 Beachcomber, July 21, 1954 and February 19, 1958.
63 Several printed accounts mistakenly place Ed King's birth year as 1865. Cumulative census records make it very clear that he was born in 1863.
64 1860 Federal Census for Georgia, Cobb County, Roswell Precinct.
65 Georgia Marriage Records from Select Counties, 1828-1978, Chatham County Marriages, Book F, 1886-1887, 292.
66 Beachcomber, undated.
67 Bill McGoun, "A Biographical History of Broward County," *Miami Herald*, 1972, 30-31.
68 Beachcomber, February 15, 1970.
69 Susan King, Fort Lauderdale Woman's Club, August 21, 1935, speaker.
70 Rodney E. Dillon, Jr. and Joe Knetsch, "Forgotten Pioneer: The Legacy of Captain William C. Valentine," *Broward Legacy* 17 (Winter/Spring 1994): 40-41.
71 Deed of Sale, dated August 22, 1895, microfilm numbers 339 and 340 from deed records provided by Dade County to Broward County for properties recorded in Dade County prior to 1915.
72 Beachcomber, November 5, 1954.

73 Beachcomber, December 10, 1959.
74 Bill McGoun, "Edwin T. King: His Handiwork Still Abundant Today," *Miami Herald*, December 12, 1971.
75 Beachcomber, September 24, 1961.
76 Mrs. Frank Oliver, "The Kings," Pioneer Days, (Fort Lauderdale) *Free Press*, June 26, 1936.
77 Beachcomber, April 30, 1959
78 Susan Gillis, 19.
79 Cooper Kirk, "The Broward County Public School System: The First Quarter Century," *Broward Legacy* 11 (Summer/Fall 1988): 26.
80 Beachcomber, October 25, 1961.
81 Beachcomber, February 16, 1970 and October 26, 1954.
82 "Transcriptions of *The Homeseeker*: a monthly publication of the Model Land Company," *Broward Legacy* 29, no.1 (2009): 9, 10.
83 Harry A. Kersey, Jr., *The Stranahans of Fort Lauderdale, a Pioneer Family of New River*, University Press of Florida, Gainesville, 2003, Chapters 3 and 4.
84 Beachcomber, January 11, 1966.
85 Beachcomber, December 22, 1954.
86 Beachcomber, November 8, 1961.
87 Deed of Sale, dated March 11, 1904, microfilm numbers 421 and 422 from deed records provided by Dade County to Broward County for properties recorded in Dade County prior to 1915.
88 Newspaper clipping, undated and unidentified source.
89 *Miami Metropolis*, July 7, 1906.
90 Beachcomber, July 7, 1955.
91 Maureen Boyce, "Lauderdale Renovation Dredges up Historic Find," *Sun Sentinel*, July 10, 1996.
92 *Edwin Thomas King and the King-Cromartie House*, Fort Lauderdale Junior League, pamphlet, 1974.
93 Beachcomber, June 25, 1958.
94 Beachcomber, April 3, 1953.
95 Beachcomber, December 4, 1953.
96 Duane Jones, "Who's Who in Broward: Mrs. B. A. Cromartie," *Miami Herald*, February 21, 1954.
97 "King-Cromartie Residence," Fort Lauderdale Historical Society, typed note.
98 "Plat of Evergreen Cemetery, Ft. Lauderdale, Fla., November 1910," Fort Lauderdale Historical Society, copy.
99 Maureen Boyce, "Final Rest: Evergreen Cemetery is Historic Final Home for Pioneers," *Sun-Sentinel*, August 4, 1996.

100 "Notes from the Stone Fields," *STONE* 32 (January-December 1911): 661-662.

101 Irving Carpenter, "B. A. Cromartie Has Lived Entire Story of Fort Lauderdale Growth," *Fort Lauderdale Times*, November 28, 1941.

102 Susan Gillis, 27.

103 *Fort Lauderdale Sentinel*, May 9, 1919.

104 Cooper Kirk, "The Broward County Public School System: The First Quarter Century," *Broward Legacy* 11 (Summer/Fall 1988): 28-30.

105 Beachcomber, October 5, 1953

106 Beachcomber, July 3, 1962.

107 Burghard and Weidling, 29-64.

108 Letter to Frank Stranahan from Ed King in Torrey Island, April 14, 1918. Fort Lauderdale Historical Society.

109 Beachcomber, September 11, 1968

110 Beachcomber, April 15, 1969

111 "The Community Saves a House," *Fort Lauderdale News*, September 14, 1971.

112 Lula Marshall Pallicer, handwritten account, Fort Lauderdale Historical Society.

113 Beachcomber, December 20, 1959.

114 "First Families of Broward: Marshall," *IMPRINTS* 16-4 (1997): 105-109.

115 Lula Marshall Pallicer, interview, Fort Lauderdale Historical Society.

116 Burghard and Weidling, 17.

117 "Mayor William Marshall Left Riverfront as Legacy," *Miami Herald*, October 24, 1971.

118 Irving Carpenter, "Marshall Can Look Back on Many Accomplishments," *Fort Lauderdale Times*, December 3, 1941.

119 Burghard and Weidling, 51.

120 Beachcomber, July 2, 1954.

121 Beachcomber, November 21, 1968.

122 "William Cabot Kyle," *New River News*, October 31, 1965.

123 "First Families of Broward: The Oliver Brothers," *IMPRINTS* 17-2 (1998): 44-46.

124 Beachcomber, August 21, 1953.

About the Author

Keith D. Mitzner, trained in counseling psychology and intelligence research and reporting, has experience in the federal bureaucracy—from analyst to executive. A genealogical researcher, Mitzner and his wife have been married more than sixty years. They have five children and nine adult grandchildren and are permanent Ft. Lauderdale residents.